THE
SIGNS AND SYMBOLS
BIBLE

THE
SIGNS AND SYMBOLS
BIBLE

THE DEFINITIVE GUIDE TO MYSTERIOUS MARKINGS

Madonna Gauding

STERLING

New York / London
www.sterlingpublishing.com

STERLING and the distinctive Sterling logo are registered trademarks
of Sterling Publishing Co., Inc.

10 9 8 7 6 5 4 3 2 1

Published by Sterling Publishing Co., Inc.
387 Park Avenue South, New York, NY 10016

First published in Great Britain in 2009, under the title
The Signs and Symbols Bible, by Godsfield Press,
an imprint of Octopus Publishing Group Ltd.
2–4 Heron Quays, London E14 4JP
© 2009 by Octopus Publishing Ltd.

Distributed in Canada by Sterling Publishing
c/o Canadian Manda Group, 165 Dufferin Street,
Toronto, Ontario, Canada M6K 3H6

Printed in China
All rights reserved

Sterling ISBN 978-1-4027-7004-3

For information about custom editions, special sales, premium and
corporate purchases, please contact Sterling Special Sales Department
at 800-805-5489 or specialsales@sterlingpublishing.com.

CONTENTS

PART ONE

INTRODUCTION

SYMBOLS, SIGNS, AND GLYPHS

A symbol is something that stands for, or represents, something other than what it is. The word "symbol" is based on the Greek verb *symballein*, meaning "to toss together" or "to join together." *Symballein* also suggests a hiding or veiling of meaning.

Symbol-making has been a deep-seated trait of humans since at least the times of the hunter-gatherers. To give an example, consider the image of an animal—a lion. The lion may be understood as the King of the Jungle and in that role it may be associated with courage, fearlessness, strength, royalty, and power. The lion is now no longer just an animal, but a symbol of many human qualities.

If it appears on a family crest, the lion may symbolize that family and its ancestors going back in time. The lion may also symbolize a king and his entire dominion. "Lion" was the nickname given to medieval rulers who had a reputation for bravery, such as Richard I of England, who was also known as Richard the Lionheart. And as guardian figures placed outside a palace, a pair of lion statues may represent superior military prowess and communicate that unlawful entry will be met with devastating attack.

As you can see, the simple image of a lion has over time become a series of ideas joined together and the lion plus its many associations is now a symbol. Given the length of time that humans have coexisted with lions, this animal has both ancient archetypal associations and symbolic meanings that are tied to specific contexts and cultures.

DECODING THE DIVINE

So, it is clear that humans make symbols in order to communicate ideas. But we also make symbols to help communicate and understand higher truths that are veiled or hidden to ordinary consciousness.

The Greek gods—each with their distinctive form and personality—were not anthropomorphic (that is, having human characteristics), but rather were symbols of a single divine being whose true nature is not personal or even comprehensible by humans. The gods functioned as symbols of qualities of the divine filtered through a human lens.

The same can be said of Buddhist deities. Tara and Yamantaka are unique figures in the Tibetan Buddhist pantheon: one male, one female, each with his or her hand implements and number of arms and heads, in an active or resting posture. Yet both represent aspects of one enlightened mind as it manifests in infinite ways.

The signs and symbols associated with the image of the Buddha communicate aspects of his enlightened nature. Those who are knowledgeable about these symbols and their meanings can look at this image and acquire a deeper insight into the human potential for enlightenment. And when Christ wears a crown, as Christ the King, Christians understand that his dominion over all creatures is an essential part of his nature and not acquired by violence; his crown does not symbolize human power, but rather the act of loving and serving others.

Lion guardian figures protect the former Royal Palace in Kathmandu, Nepal, which today is a museum.

White Tara, the goddess of compassion in Tibetan Buddhism, is often associated with the symbol of the lotus.

Symbols speak in layers of meaning and provide a shorthand for different ideas. Divine figures and images are human attempts to symbolize the ineffable—that which cannot be expressed in words. They also present the surface of that which is hidden and veiled, which may require deeper exploration.

POINTING THE WAY

Whereas a symbol always stands for something more than its immediate meaning and challenges us to go beyond the surface, to discover rich, expansive layers of significance, a sign points the way. A lion may symbolize many ideas and qualities that cannot necessarily be put into words, whereas an image of a lion (together with an arrow) at the zoo probably points the way to the lion cages —and is a sign. Some things, such as a wedding ring, can function as both sign and symbol. A ring is a sign that the person wearing it is married and it is a symbol of any number of ideas, such as fidelity, love, romance, and devotion.

Its circular shape symbolizes eternal love with no beginning and no end.

Glyphs are picture symbols that represent an object or concept, and they fall somewhere between a sign and a symbol. They differ from symbols in that they are usually more graphic and less prone to varying interpretations, yet they communicate more meaning than signs. In contemporary culture, a crossed red circle superimposed on a picture of a dog is a glyph representing the simple idea that dogs (and perhaps other pets) are not welcome. Whole early written languages, such as Egyptian hieroglyphs, were based on glyphs or pictograms.

The Egyptian hieroglyphic language was based on glyphs or pictograms.

ARCHETYPES

Carl Jung (1875–1961), the Swiss psychiatrist and founder of analytical psychology, believed that looking at symbol creation would provide a key to understanding human nature. A symbol, as defined by Jung, is the best possible expression of something that is essentially difficult to explain or know. Investigating the symbols of religious, mythological, and magical systems from many cultures and time periods, he discovered remarkable similarities. To account for these, Jung suggested that the unconscious is divided into two layers. The first layer of the unconscious, which he called the personal unconscious, is the reservoir of material

Swiss psychiatrist Carl Jung used symbols and archetypes as keys to understanding human nature.

acquired by an individual through his or her life that he or she has mostly forgotten or repressed.

The second layer of the unconscious, which Jung named the collective unconscious, contains the cellular memories that are common to all of humankind. These common memories and experiences form archetypes—or primordial, symbolic images that reflect basic patterns and universal themes that are common to all peoples.

UNIVERSAL ARCHETYPES

Archetypes exist outside of space and time. Examples of archetypes identified by Jung are the Shadow, the Old Wise Person, the Anima, the Animus, the Trickster, the Mother, the Father, and the Innocent Child. There are also many nature archetypes that are common to all people, such as fire, ocean, river, mountain, sky, and tree. Gods and goddesses and the heroes and heroines of world myths also function as archetypes.

Jung discovered that, because of the collective unconscious, humans have a disposition to react to life in the same way as the human beings who have gone before. He discovered patterns which are distinctly human that structure our minds and imaginations. This pattern is realized when an image from the collective

ARCHETYPES IN *HARRY POTTER*

The *Harry Potter* series of novels is filled with archetypal images, which partly explains its unprecedented worldwide popularity. Through the narrative arc of the seven books, Harry Potter embodies a range of archetypes, from the Orphan and the Lost Soul to the Hero and the Warrior; as the Hero and the Warrior he is courageous, focused, loyal, strong, and capable.

Providing worldly wisdom, emotional grounding, moral and ethical principles, and discipline, Professor Dumbledore can be seen as an embodiment of the archetype of the Father or the Patriarch. In contrast, Hagrid embodies the archetype of the Wild Man in his love of freedom, his connection with nature and animals, and his rejection of the comforts of ordinary civilization.

unconscious enters the consciousness of a person in some way, such as through dreams or myths. For example, the Old Wise Person may appear in the dreams of three different people, featuring as a loving grandmother in Kansas in one dream, as a tramp on the street in London in another, and as an old woman healer in Africa in a third. Despite the differences, for each person the dream still refers back to the archetype of the Old Wise Person. Archetypes and archetypal images also appear in novels, films, music, and plays.

Jung postulated that, as human beings, we share in a single Universal Unconscious, the collective unconscious. And he believed that even the first layer of the unconscious, the personal unconscious, is shaped according to patterns that are universal. Learning about symbols helps us to have greater awareness and power in our own lives.

Because of inborn ways of perceiving the world, and our shared unconscious material, many of the symbols that are collected in this book may have a powerful influence on us without us necessarily even thinking consciously about them. Advertisers, for instance, use archetypal symbols to great effect in selling their products. A good example is the Marlboro Man, a Wild Man symbol in the form of the American cowboy. The Leo Burnett advertising agency created this hyper-masculine figure to sell filtered cigarettes to GIs returning from the Second World War, who were used to smoking unfiltered cigarettes and thought of filtered cigarettes as effeminate.

HIDDEN KNOWLEDGE

As Jung has so eloquently proved, symbols are not only the language of the unconscious, but also of the occult. The word "occult" comes from the Latin *occultus*, meaning "hidden" and therefore refers to "knowledge of the hidden."

In the English language this means "knowledge of the paranormal," as opposed to knowledge obtained as a result of science. The occult relates to the study of a deeper spiritual reality that extends beyond pure reason and the physical sciences. The term is also used as a label that is given to a number of mystical organizations or orders, such as the alchemists and those who practiced ceremonial witchcraft, and to the teachings and practices as taught by them. The name also extends to a large body of literature and spiritual philosophy.

Many of the symbols in this book refer to hidden spiritual knowledge, both Eastern and Western. In later life Jung added to his theories by suggesting that the deepest levels of the unconscious touched on the paranormal and lay outside the bounds of time, space, and causality. This level was both of and beyond Universal Consciousness. It was this deeper level that held the promise of spiritual realization and the possibility of enlightenment.

Alchemists pursued hidden knowledge and spiritual enlightenment through their attempts to turn ordinary base metals into gold.

ABOUT THIS BOOK

There is never unanimity over the meaning and representation of symbols, but the descriptions in this book reflect the most commonly held interpretations. Some symbols are ancient and have changed form over time; different versions of them may exist. But the differences do not take away from their archetypal power.

The world of symbols is dynamic and changes as knowledge and customs change. Yet symbols retain aspects of universal wisdom and meaning to which humans have responded throughout time, and continue to respond. As you will discover in the following pages, the history of symbolism shows that everything can assume symbolic significance:

• Natural objects (such as stones, plants, animals, mountains, valleys, the sun, and the moon)

• Man-made things (such as temples, houses, tools, ritual items, and calendars)

• Abstract forms (such as shapes, colors, and numbers).

Everything in the cosmos becomes a potential symbol, because humans unconsciously transform objects or images into symbols and thereby endow them with great psychological or religious importance. The confluence of religion and art, reaching back into prehistoric times, has left a record of those symbols that were meaningful to our ancestors.

This book collects symbols from ancient civilizations (pages 22–67), from Western and Middle Eastern religions (pages 68–107), and from the Eastern religions (pages 108–159). It covers secular and religious symbols of power (pages 160–175), of heraldry (pages 176–185), and of alchemy, astrology, and ceremonial magic (pages 186–229). It describes the symbols of the natural world: animals (pages 230–279), plants (pages 280–309), and minerals, crystals, and gemstones (pages 310–331). It also collects amulet and talisman symbols (pages 332–349), letter symbols (pages 350–365), and symbols relating to time, shape, number, and color (pages 366–391).

READING THE SYMBOLS

Wherever you are, you are wrapped in symbols. This book will increase your awareness of symbols as they appear in your everyday life, opening you to an intense experience of meaning as you travel throughout your day. All forms of art (including music, architecture, sculpture, and painting) and all forms of literature and moving images (including novels, plays, poetry, films, and television shows) are filled with symbolic meaning. Many advertisements (in both print and television) use symbolism in subtle ways. Viewing them with a critical eye can be interesting and enlightening, so use this book to learn about the symbols that you will now begin to see all around you.

The star and crescents on this mosque are symbols of the Islamic faith.

The mother archetype is symbolized in the myth of Demeter and Persephone.

Paying attention to your dreams, and writing them down every morning, will give you insight into what the archetypal images are trying to tell you. Dream symbols can be powerfully transformative if you make the effort to become conscious of them and work with them.

When visiting a museum or art gallery, take this book along for reference. The artist may or may not have been conscious of the symbols that appear in his or her work. If interesting objects or figures emerge, explore their symbolic meaning to enhance your experience. If you are viewing ancient or medieval art, the symbols will usually be found in this book.

Once you have read this book, you will notice how various symbols are used every time you see a film or read a novel. In your daily life you will be able to work with symbols to consciously embody the energies and meanings that are important to you. When deciding what sort of flowers to send to a friend, for example, you can select those that symbolize the deeper meaning you wish to communicate. You can choose to wear a particular gemstone for its special healing and energetic qualities and for what it stands for in your life. When decorating your home, you can select art objects, paintings, and furnishings that include the symbols with which you would like to surround yourself. If you choose a statue of the Buddha, you will be able to understand the spiritual meaning symbolized by its various aspects.

You can read this book through from cover to cover or simply keep it for reference, looking up symbols as you go. Either way, the following chapters are your key to the secret, potent, healing world of symbols.

Symbols shown in Carlo Crivelli's Annunciation with St. Emidius *(1486) include a peacock, the Christian symbol of eternity and immortality, and a gherkin and apple used as the artist's signature.*

PART 2

SYMBOLS DIRECTORY

ANCIENT CIVILIZATIONS

Some symbols can be traced back to ancient civilizations when humans used them both to communicate and to represent the world in which they lived and died. They developed systems to study the sun, moon, and stars, and sophisticated cosmologies to explain the origin of the universe. Living in a world that was mysterious and unpredictable, they identified a pantheon of archetypal gods and goddesses. From them they sought both protection and blessings, and through them accessed the ineffable—those divine truths and realizations beyond the limitations of the ordinary human mind.

THE EGYPTIANS

The unification of Upper and Lower Egypt, in around 3200 BCE, gave rise to dynastic Egypt, one of the oldest civilizations in the world, which flourished for more than 4,000 years. Because it flooded annually, the Nile River made the land surrounding it extremely fertile, which enabled the ancient Egyptians to cultivate wheat and other crops. Many Egyptian symbols are rooted in the extremes of the natural environment and in the gods and goddesses thought to influence the natural world and the afterlife. The individual glyphs of the ancient Egyptian pictographic writing system often became symbols that functioned as powerful talismans and amulets.

HEART

Egyptians believed the heart to be the center of the human being and the seat of wisdom and intelligence. Considered essential for life in eternity, the heart was the only organ left in the body after mummification. At death, it was believed that the gods conducted a sacred ceremony during which the heart was weighed against a feather. Maat, the goddess of truth and justice, held the scales. If the scales balanced, the deceased would be invited to enter the underworld. If the heart weighed more than the feather, a monster would devour it.

EYE OF HORUS

Known as *wadjet*, the Eye of Horus represents the left eye of the Egyptian falcon-headed god Horus. As the story goes, Horus's eye was ripped out when he battled his uncle Set to avenge the murder of his father, Osiris. The eye was cast into the sky and became associated with the moon. Troth, the god of the moon, healed the injured eye. From the dark of the moon the eye took 29 days to heal and at the full moon the eye was whole again. Out of love, Horus offered his healed eye to his dead father, Osiris, helping to bring him back to life. Thus the Eye of Horus symbolizes sacrifice, wholeness, and restorative power.

In many parts of the world today this symbol of the sound eye, or the "good eye," is worn as an amulet to bring protection from the "evil eye"—an intrusive, covetous gaze from another person (see page 335). The Eye of Horus can still be found painted on the prow of fishing boats in Mediterranean countries.

ANKH

The ankh held numerous meanings for the ancient Egyptians; many focused on the concept of "life." The ankh represents the life-sustaining elements of water and air, as well as sexual reproduction, death, and the afterlife. In Egyptian paintings, gods hold ankh symbols to the noses of pharaohs or queens, symbolizing air as the breath of eternal life. Streams of ankh signs flow down over the monarchs, representing the flow of life-giving water. As a symbol of fertility, the loop of the ankh represents the vagina, and the line below stands for the penis in union with it.

On a spiritual level, the ankh symbolizes the key to hidden knowledge. The loop of the ankh also stands for the eternal soul that has no beginning or end, and the cross represents the actual state of death. The ankh signifies the spiritual initiation that one must go through in order to open the gates of the Kingdom of the Dead and penetrate the meaning of eternal life. The Christian Coptic cross, which is also known as the Gnostic cross, has its origin in the Egyptian ankh.

FETISH

The Egyptian fetish is a stuffed, headless animal skin (usually a great cat or a bull). It is associated with embalming and with the gods Imiut, Anubis, and Osiris. The fetish, sometimes with a papyrus or lotus blossom attached to its tail, was hung on a pole and then planted in a pot. It symbolized magical powers captured from the gods for use during funerary rites. Man-made replicas of the fetish crafted out of precious metals have been found in the tombs of the pharaohs.

NEBU

The Egyptian symbol of gold was the nebu, a collar made of gold with beads hanging along its lower edge. Gold was considered by the Egyptians to be the actual flesh of the gods and was especially associated with the sun god Ra and his daughter, the goddess Hathor. A divine and imperishable substance, gold symbolized the brilliance of the sun. Incapable of being tarnished, it represented the hope of eternal life. Isis, the goddess who protects the dead, is often depicted kneeling on a nebu, the hieroglyphic sign for gold.

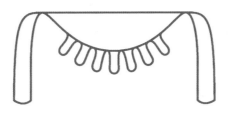

PALM BRANCH

The palm branch was a practical time-keeping device and a symbol of astrology. Through close observation of the heavens, the Egyptians developed a sophisticated 365-day calendar. They kept track of the days, months, and years by placing notches on palm branches, which were also a symbol of longevity. Seshat, the goddess of writing and measurement, was often portrayed holding a notched palm branch on which she calculated the earthly life of the king.

TYET

The tyet—which is also known as the Knot of Isis, the Girdle of Isis, and the Blood of Isis—is an ancient Egyptian symbol of the goddess Isis. It looks similar to the ankh (see page 26), except its arms curve down to resemble the knot that fastens the garments of gods and goddesses. Like the loop of the ankh, the loop of the tyet refers to eternal life, but more specifically to the inexhaustible life force of the goddess Isis from whom all life flows. When made of a red semi-precious stone or glass, the tyet was known as the Blood of Isis, representing the menstrual blood flowing from Isis's womb, bestowing its magical powers and protection on the one who carries the amulet.

Like the ankh, the Knot of Isis is about immortality, but it is also about the spiritual journey that is necessary to realize this state. It reminds the spiritual seeker that he or she has to unravel the knots that bind one to ordinary life, in order to be free to experience the joys of eternity.

SCARAB

The ancient Egyptians worshipped the scarab, or dung beetle, as an embodiment of Khepri, the god who maintained the movement of the sun. Khepri is sometimes depicted as a beetle or as a man with a beetle's head. For the Egyptians, the scarab symbolized resurrection and new life. The scarab's rolling of a round ball of dung across the ground was thought to imitate the journey of the sun through the sky. In Egyptian paintings the scarab beetle may be depicted carrying a huge sun on its back.

Because the scarab beetle often lays its eggs in the bodies of dead animals, the ancient Egyptians believed that it was created from dead matter or from the primordial ooze itself. Thus it symbolized the creation of life. Both the god Khepri and the scarab are associated with rebirth, renewal, and resurrection—Khepri's name means "to come into being." Scarabs are sometimes painted with outstretched falcon wings, symbolizing their role in protection. The carved-stone scarab figure was a popular protective amulet in Egypt.

PAPYRUS

Throughout ancient Egypt, tall papyrus plants covered the marshes of the Nile Delta. The Egyptians depended on this plant to make everyday objects such as boats, mattresses, and paper. Thus the papyrus was both a natural symbol of life itself and of the primeval marsh from which it came.

As a perennial, the papyrus symbolized joy, youth, and yearly renewal. Papyrus plants, which could grow up to 10 feet (3 meters) high, were thought to hold up the sky and consequently many temples were built with papyrus-shaped columns. During the Old Kingdom, the papyrus served as a symbol of Lower Egypt, while the lotus symbolized Upper Egypt.

In hieroglyphics, the papyrus roll had royal connotations and also signified the book and knowledge. To make papyrus rolls, strips of papyrus pith were laid at right angles on top of each other and pasted together. The rolling and unrolling of the papyrus symbolized two aspects of knowledge: that which was meant for everyone and that which was meant for an inner circle of spiritual initiates. So important was the papyrus plant to the Egyptians that goddesses were depicted holding a stalk as a magical scepter.

SHEN

This hieroglyphic representation of a doubled rope with its ends tied in a straight line, with no beginning or end, was a symbol of eternity, and it also signified protection. It is frequently associated with representations of Heh, the god of eternity, and often forms the base of the notched palm branches (see page 27) held by gods and goddesses, indicating their connection to eternal life.

Sometimes the Shen is depicted with a sun at its center, symbolizing its solar aspect. In Egyptian paintings, deities in bird form—such as Horus the falcon (see page 260) and Mut the vulture—are shown holding the Shen in their claws.

The word comes from the Egyptian *shenu*, meaning "to encircle." In its elongated form, the Shen became a cartouche indicating that the enclosed hieroglyphics referred to a pharaoh or other important figure who was under divine protection. The cartouche symbolized everything that the sun's rays touched, indicating that the king ruled the entire cosmos. The cartouche hieroglyph also appeared on gold finger rings and decorating cartouche-shaped boxes.

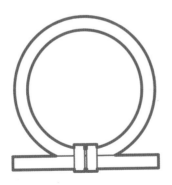

SISTRUM

The sistrum, a sacred musical instrument of ancient Egypt, has a frame with small discs that rattle when the instrument is shaken by hand. The basic outline often resembles the ankh (see page 26), symbolizing life. The head of the goddess Hathor is often depicted on the handle, although the sistrum is also associated with Bast, the goddess of dance and joy. The instrument produced a soft, jangling sound, resembling a breeze blowing through papyrus reeds, a sound that was said to please and placate the gods and goddesses. It was shaken in short, rhythmic pulses to arouse ecstatic movement for religious processions and ceremonies relating mainly to Hathor.

Many of the sistrums in museum collections are inscribed with the names of royal persons and sistrums are depicted in paintings in the hands of royal family members. In Late Period paintings, the sistrum is shown held by priestesses of the Hathor cult as they adore the deity face to face. Such intimacy with a god was a female prerogative and use of the sistrum seems to have carried erotic or fertility connotations allied with the cult of Hathor.

DJEW

The Djew, the hieroglyphic sign for mountain, depicts two peaks with a valley running between them. The Egyptians believed that a cosmic mountain range with two peaks named Manu and Bakhu held up the heavens. The double lion god Aker guarded the peaks and protected the sun as it rose and set. The Djew was also a symbol of the tomb and the afterlife, probably because most Egyptian tombs were located in mountainous areas.

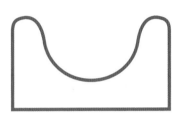

AKHET

The Akhet, the hieroglyphic sign for the horizon, is similar to the two peaks of the Djew, but with a solar disc cradled between them. It symbolized sunrise and sunset. For Egyptians, the day began at sunrise, when the goddess Nut gave birth to the sun in her daily affirmation of the triumph of life over death. The sun was thought to sail across the cosmic sky in a boat during the day. It would sink below the horizon at night, to face the demons of the underworld, only to rise again in the morning. As such, the Akhet symbolizes the daily promise of hope and renewal.

THE MESOPOTAMIANS

The early Mesopotamian empires of Sumeria, Assyria, and Babylon are often referred to as the "cradle of civilization." The convergence of the Tigris and Euphrates Rivers, in what is now Iraq, produced rich, fertile soil and a supply of water that enabled the growth of agriculture and urban settlements. These settlements started with a collection of houses surrounding a ziggurat, a ceremonial pyramid used for worshipping the divine. In time, these became sophisticated cities that practiced agriculture and developed written languages and systems of astronomy and mathematics. Many of the symbols of ancient Assyria and Sumeria revolved around worship of the goddess Ishtar, or Inanna, who symbolized the capricious and primal forces of nature that can both create and destroy crops and life.

ISHTAR

The Assyrian moon goddess associated with both fertility and destruction, Ishtar was the most important female deity in Mesopotamia and is associated with many symbols. In her sacred sexual aspect, she is depicted as a nude figure wearing a horned cap with a cone symbolizing the cosmic mountain and an eight-pointed star symbolizing the planet Venus. Her wings designate her status as a stellar goddess.

A crescent worn on her head symbolizes her link to the moon and her seven-colored necklace represents the seven gates of the underworld. Her girdle depicts the constellations of the zodiac. Wild and savage, Ishtar was known for her unbridled sexuality and love of war. She is usually represented as an armed warrior, sometimes shown riding a lion or standing on a pair of lions.

ZIGGURAT

Common to the Sumerians, Babylonians, and Assyrians of ancient Mesopotamia, the temple structures known as ziggurats first appeared in Babylonia around the 3rd millennium BCE. A ziggurat had a square base and was made up of a series of increasingly narrow terraces linked by steep flights of stairs. The ziggurats had up to seven terraces, each painted a different color, symbolizing the different planetary heavens. The base represented Saturn and was painted black. The second level was painted orange, to signify Jupiter. The third was painted red, for Mars. The fourth was golden, for the sun. The fifth was light yellow, for Venus. The sixth was painted blue, to represent Mercury. And the seventh level was silver, signifying the moon. On the top level, priests conducted ceremonies in which sacrifices were made to the gods.

These huge towers were a physical symbol of the enormous need and desire that humans have for connecting with the divine. They were intended to provide a link between heaven and earth and to facilitate the connection between gods and humans. Climbing the ziggurat symbolized the journey from the mundane to the transcendent.

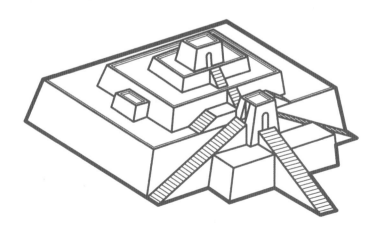

THE TREE OF LIFE

This symbol, which is found in nearly every culture, is a visual representation of the link between the three worlds: heaven, earth, and the underworld. The Assyrian Tree of Life, the oldest and most famous of all sacred trees, is associated with worship of the goddess Ishtar (see page 34). It first appeared on Chaldean cylinders as a pillar crossed by branches and topped by a crescent. The pillar symbolized the human spinal cord or the World Spine. Later, in around the 10th century BCE, the tree became more complex and elegant, with curved branches, scrollwork, and beautiful seven-petaled flower forms.

In Babylonia, the Tree of Life was known as a magical tree that grew in the center of paradise. The Babylonian, Egyptian, Islamic, and Kabbalistic Tree of Life (see page 75), as well as the biblical Tree of Paradise, evolved directly from the ancient Assyrian tree symbol. In all cultures, the Tree of Life is a symbol of reproduction. The serpent and bird, representing the union of matter and spirit, also are associated with the Tree of Life.

NISROCH

The Assyrian god Nisroch was an eagle-headed deity with wings and a body-builder physique. His imposing masculine form represented the absolute power of the king and of the gods. His swift flight and powerful vision symbolized the connection between heaven and earth and between the spiritual and ordinary worlds. In his left hand he holds a water vessel for watering the sacred Tree of Life (see page 37). This activity symbolized the protection of the land to ensure the royal power of the king and the prosperity of the invincible Assyrian nation.

Nisroch was the beloved god of the Assyrian King Sennacherib who reigned from 704 to 681 BCE and it was in his temple that Sennacherib was murdered by two of his sons. Some scholars have suggested that Nisroch is a representation of Asshur, the patriarch and head of the Assyrian pantheon.

WINGED SPHINX

The Assyrian sphinx, a winged lion with a human head, symbolized royal power. The lion's body represented strength, the wings warned of a swift and ferocious response to attack, and the masculine head symbolized royalty. In the form of large stone sculptures, these supernatural beings guarded palace entrances and intimidated invaders as a symbol of overwhelming strength. In addition to warding off potential attackers, sphinxes repelled evil forces and negative energy directed at the king. (See also page 276.)

MARDUK

The Mesopotamian winged-bull deities symbolized masculine power, protection, authority, and the qualities of potency and virility. The deity Marduk appears as a winged bull with a male human face. He gained his patriarchal power by defeating the goddess Tiamat, known as the Dragoness of Chaos and the Primeval Mother of All. Upon his victory he gained 50 names of power. He is known as a Master of Magic, who can banish demons and convey positive energy through the magical use of water. He is a god of healing, regeneration, and light, and a firm enforcer of the law.

THE GREEKS AND ROMANS

Early Greeks and Romans created a civilization that remains the foundation of the Western world today. Their political systems, law, technology, art, literature, and language continue to have immense influence on modern Western culture. Greek and Roman religion was polytheistic (worshipping more than one god), and each of the many gods and goddesses expressed archetypal qualities that still find expression today in theater, literature, and film. Other symbols, such as the Roman cornucopia (the horn of plenty), have survived unchanged. The cornucopia has communicated through the ages a complex set of ideas about harvest, plenty, aspirations for wealth and security, thanksgiving for material wealth, and the joys of celebration, food, and family.

ASCLEPIUS WAND

In ancient Greek mythology, Asclepius, the god of healing, was a practitioner of medicine. The symbol of the wand or rod of Asclepius is associated with astrology and the practice of medicine and consists of a single serpent entwined around a staff. The serpent, which is shedding its skin, is a symbol of rebirth and fertility, while the staff is a symbol of the authority of the god of medicine. Asclepius was so skilled as a healer that he was reputed to have brought patients back from the dead.

CADUCEUS

A winged rod with two snakes wrapped around it, the caduceus is an ancient astrological symbol associated with the Greek god Hermes. It was used by the astrologer-priests in the Eleusinian Mysteries and has since been associated with Gnostic practices and with kundalini yoga. The caduceus is thought to be a symbolic representation of the subtle nerve channels that run up the spine. In the 7th century CE it became associated with astrological medicine and it remains a symbol of medical and pharmaceutical practice today.

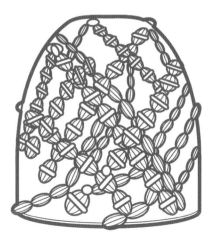

OMPHALOS

The omphalos, meaning "navel stone," is a symbol of the center of the world. According to ancient Greek myth, Zeus sent out two eagles to fly in different directions across the world. Where they met would determine the world's "navel," or center. Omphalos stones used to mark this mythical point were erected in several places around the Mediterranean, the most famous being at Delphi. The omphalos stone may have originated with the "stone of splendor" associated with the Canaanite god Baal and was said to facilitate communication with the gods.

LAUREL WREATH

A laurel wreath is a circular band made of branches and leaves of the fragrant bay laurel plant. In Greek mythology, laurel symbolizes Apollo, who wears a laurel wreath on his head (see page 285). The Greeks call laurel *dhafni* because it is also associated with the goddess Daphne. In ancient Greece, wreaths were awarded to victors of the Olympics, poetic contests, and military conquests and so the laurel wreath is often seen as a symbol of victory. The term "poet laureate" has its origin in this ancient Greek practice.

SCALES OF JUSTICE

The scales of justice are associated with Themis, the Greek goddess of divine justice, one of the first oracles at Delphi and an adviser to the god Zeus. She is depicted holding the scales of justice in one hand and a sword in the other, and is sometimes wearing a blindfold. The scales symbolize the weighing of actions and the fair and balanced administration of the law without prejudice. They also represent the imposing of order and control over the affairs of gods and humans.

PEARL

The pearl—pale, shimmering, lunar, feminine, and born in the ocean within the confines of a shell—is associated with hidden knowledge and esoteric wisdom. For the ancient Greeks, pearls were also symbols of love and marriage. The pearl's likeness to a fetus in the womb made it a symbol of the generative powers of the feminine. Also, the pearl symbolized the ideal person of the Greek philosopher Plato (c. 428–c. 348 BCE), who required transformation in order to attain perfection. (See also page 330.)

BEE

In Greek mythology, the bee was a symbol of the soul and was thought to provide a bridge from the natural world to the underworld. The bee was associated with the goddess Demeter and with her daughter Persephone's descent into the underworld. In nature, the bee would seem to disappear in the winter only to return in the spring, and so it became a symbol of resurrection and rebirth. This sacred insect appeared as decoration on tombs as a symbol of the afterlife and some tombs were even made in the shape of beehives. (See also page 251.)

CERBERUS

Cerberus is the monstrous three-headed dog of Greek mythology. He is said to guard the gates of the underworld (Hades), barring the living from entering and ensuring that the spirits of the dead could enter, but not exit. Hades consisted of several realms, including the Elysian Fields (heaven) and Tartarus (hell).

Cerberus, or the Hound of Hades, symbolized a person's fear of the actual hell realms, as well as of the hell realms that exist within one's own psyche. This internal demon had to be conquered by relying on one's own efforts. The god Heracles tamed Cerberus with the spiritual power of music.

HERCULES KNOT

The knot of Hercules, created with two intertwined cords, originated as a wedding symbol in ancient Greece. It represented the knotted belt, a symbol of virginity that is worn by the bride and untied by the groom during the ceremony; this custom is the origin of the phrase "tying the knot." The knot symbolized the potency of the god Hercules and the legendary "girdle of Diana" captured from the Amazonian Queen Hippolyta. It was also used as a love amulet.

CUPID

Cupid was the Roman god of love, similar to the Greek god Eros. He is depicted as a winged boy, nude, or sometimes wearing a diaper, holding a bow and a quiver of arrows. He symbolizes youth, fickleness, and romantic love. He has two sets of arrows: one with gold arrowheads, used to inspire love in the person whose heart he pierces, and the other with lead arrowheads, which provoke hatred. Often he is shown blindfolded, signifying that love is blind.

MEDUSA

According to Greek myth, Athene (also spelled Athena) cursed Medusa because of a sexual transgression, causing anyone who looked upon her to be turned to stone. In reality, Medusa was an early serpent goddess, who was worshipped by the women of Lybia and represented female wisdom. She was the destroyer aspect of the Triple Goddess (see page 103) called Neith in Egypt and Athene in North Africa. During the pre-Hellenic period (approximately 2000–1150 BCE), Athene wore the image of Medusa on her breastplate, an indication that she and Medusa were one. However, later classical Greek myth erased the ancient female-wisdom connections of Athene and instead depicted her as an expression of Zeus's wisdom and as having been born out of his head.

CORNUCOPIA

The cornucopia, or horn of plenty, was a symbol of generosity, fruitfulness, and happiness in ancient Greek and Roman culture. The cornucopia was associated with many deities, including Copia (goddess of abundance), Bacchus (god of wine), Ceres (goddess of agriculture), and Achelous (the river god), and represented the gifts they bestowed on humans. Later, the cornucopia took on the additional connotations of hard work and foresight resulting in the public good, the bounty of the harvest, and the prosperity of all.

TRISKELION

The triskelion, from the Greek word meaning "three-legged," is one of the oldest symbols known to humankind. The three legs emerging from a central point, representing power, energy, and forward motion, can be found on prehistoric rock carvings in northern Italy, on Greek coins and vases from the 6th century BCE, and on earlier Mycenean pottery. The version of the triskelion that is a symbol of Sicily has the head of Medusa (see opposite) in the center. Pliny the Elder said that the triskelion represented the triangular shape of the island and its three bays.

MINOTAUR

This symbol has its origins in the story of Cretan Minos. Wanting to be king, he prayed to Poseidon to send him a snow-white bull as a sign of his approval. A beautiful white bull appeared, but Minos did not sacrifice it as promised. When Poseidon learned about Minos's deception, he made Minos's wife, Pasipha, fall madly in love with the bull. Their offspring was a monster called the Minotaur, which had the head and tail of a bull on the body of a man. The Minotaur, who was killed by Theseus, represents the human struggle with one's animal nature.

LABYRS

The labyrs, or "double axe," symbol was the emblem of Minoan goddesses, who were depicted holding one in each hand. The labyrs represented a butterfly, as a symbol of transformation and rebirth. The palace of Knossos was known as the Labyrinth, or the House of the Double Axe, and the labyrs symbol was used extensively as a decorative element in the palace itself. This symbol of the Great Goddess was not intended as a weapon, as it predated the appearance of metal axes by thousands of years.

LABYRINTH

Minos created a labyrinth in which to imprison the Minotaur (see opposite) and every year he locked up seven youths and maidens there for the Minotaur to feast upon. When the hero Theseus learned of these sacrifices, he posed as one of the youths in order to save them. Ariadne, Minos's daughter, fell in love with Theseus and gave him a ball of thread to unravel as he entered the labyrinth. Theseus slayed the sleeping Minotaur at the center, then led the others to safety by following the thread back to the entrance. The labyrinth symbolizes a journey to the interior of one's soul or psyche. (See also page 374.)

THE CELTS

The Celts, an Indo-European people, inhabited large parts of central Europe, Spain, Ireland, and Britain between the 5th and 1st centuries BCE. They were animists, believing that everything in the natural world contained spirits, or divine entities, with which humans could establish a relationship. Unlike Greek and Roman culture, Celtic society was predominantly rural and tribal. Power in life came from the otherworld, which was the realm of ancestors and the dead and the dwelling place of the gods and other spirits. Many animals were considered sacred by the Celts and trees were believed to have special powers. Celtic symbols reflect a deep connection to the patterns and energies of the natural world.

LOZENGE

The lozenge is an ancient Celtic female symbol that represents the vulva or womb of the Great Mother. On the feast of St. Brigid (February 1), women in parts of Ireland today still make St. Brigid's cross, an amulet that consists of a diamond-shaped lozenge of straw woven around a little wooden cross. Every year the crosses are blessed by priests and hung in houses for protection against fire and lightning. They are also placed in stables for protection of the animals. St. Brigid is the direct descendant of the pre-Christian goddess Brighid.

CELTIC CROSS

The Celtic cross—today drawn as a cross superimposed on a circle—has its roots in the pre-Christian, pagan era dating back to 5000 BCE. Although its exact origins are unknown, it may be an early symbol of the Celtic sun god Taranis. In the earliest periods, the cross was drawn entirely within the circle and was without decoration. Later, the cross became larger, the arms were extended and both circle and cross were covered with elaborate decorative elements, including knots, spirals, and key patterns (see pages 52–53).

As a pagan symbol, the Celtic cross combines the female circle and the male cross to form an image of fertility and sexual union. The cross was associated with the four cardinal points of the compass and the flow of time; the circle with the cycles of death and rebirth; and the center—where time stands still—with the point of entry into the underworld.

The Celtic cross became an emblem of the Church when the Celts converted to Christianity. The cross then symbolized the Crucifixion and the circle stood for Christ's resurrection and eternal life. (See also page 377.)

CELTIC SPIRALS

Spirals are found in every aspect of nature, from magnetic fields to spiral galaxies and the inner ear (see also page 375). Plants and shells grow in spiral formations and Mother Nature releases her fury in the spiral of the tornado and the hurricane. The Celtic peoples and their ancestors used the spiral to represent the natural world and the spiritual mysteries of life.

The three-pronged Spiral of Life at the entrance to the megalithic passage tomb at Newgrange in Ireland symbolized the sacred cycle of birth, death, and rebirth. The initiate would walk round the spiral-marked barrier into the labyrinth sanctuary and then follow the path to its center; there, heaven and earth were joined.

The Celtic triskelion (see also page 47), a three-pronged spiral within a circle, is also said to represent the Triple Goddess (see page 103) and our triple relationship with the earth, our self, and the divine.

CHEVRON

The chevron, a masculine symbol, resembled the arrowheads used by Celtic warriors and represented high rank and military power. It may have represented the shape of a rafter in a building. In ancient Celtic art, the chevron is repeated in bands, forming borders and/or other ornamentation. A simplified form of the chevron, a V shape, is used in contemporary military insignia to indicate rank or length of service.

KEY PATTERNS

Celtic key patterns are interlocking angular key shapes that are, in effect, straightened spirals. The paths formed by the pattern are constructed on a diagonal grid and turn back on themselves at various angles, symbolizing the winding path of the labyrinth (see page 374). The key pattern suggests a spiritual journey during which the seeker simultaneously moves toward his or her spiritual center and that of the universe. At the center of the labyrinth, called the "navel" or omphalos (see page 41), heaven, earth, and self are experienced as one.

CELTIC KNOT

A Celtic knot forms a complete loop with no beginning and no end. Celtic knots may be simple or highly complex and are found on crosses, structures, manuscripts, and other artifacts throughout the Celtic world. Celtic zoomorphic (animal) designs are similar in construction, but the cords terminate in feet, heads, or tails. The intricate looping of knot patterns suggests the interconnectedness of all life, eternity, and the mysteries of birth, death, and reincarnation. The interwoven figures of people and animals signify the intimate connection that the Celts had with the natural world. Some knots were used as magical talismans for protection against earthly threats and evil spirits.

GREEN MAN

The Celtic Green Man, a god of the plant world, is associated with the Celtic belief that gods and spirits lived in trees. His leaf-covered face symbolizes humanity's dependence on the abundance of nature, and the power of the plant world to sustain and renew life. A joyful figure, he was widely celebrated during spring fertility festivals. Carvings of the Green Man were also used for protection from malevolent spirits.

CERNUNNOS

Cernunnos was a male hunter god associated with the reproduction of the forest and with horned animals, such as the stag and ram-headed snake. He was also called Lord of the Animals, the Horned Sacred One, and Lord of the Hunt. He is depicted as a horned man seated cross-legged, sometimes holding a snake. His antlers symbolize the yearly cycle of death, regeneration, and renewal, as does his snake, which sheds its skin. He wears a torc, an ornate necklace used to denote nobility, and carries another torc or a purse filled with coins symbolizing wealth and commerce.

CAULDRON

In Celtic lore there are many types of cauldrons. One of these, called the horn of plenty (see page 47), is associated with the god Dagda and provided both bodily sustenance and knowledge of the arts and sciences. Another was the cauldron of Mabinogi of Branwen, in which the dead were placed to be reborn. A third was the cauldron of the goddess Kerriwen, patron of poets, smiths, and physicians, who used hers as a source of magical powers and inspiration.

SHEELA-NA-GIG

Often found above church doorways and windows, Sheela-na-Gig is a carved representation of a naked woman with her legs apart, displaying an oversized vulva or yoni (see page 111). Some believe Sheela-na-Gig represents a pre-Christian pagan goddess, perhaps a fertility figure. Another theory is that she protected against evil. The carvings closely resemble yonic versions of the Hindu goddess Kali (see page 118), placed above the doors of homes in India for protection. Sheela-na-Gig may depict Kali's Celtic manifestation, Caillech or Old Woman, a goddess in her crone or destroyer aspect, from whose vulva all life emerges and returns.

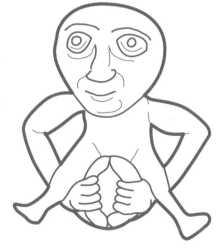

THE SCANDINAVIANS

Gods worshipped by the Norse warriors—the Vikings—included Odin (god of memory and thought), Thor (god of thunder and lightning), Freya (goddess of love and beauty), and Greyr (horned god of fertility). The Vikings also used the longboat as a symbol of speed and supremacy to terrorize their enemies, and in burial rituals as an emblem of the journey to the afterlife. Early Scandinavians also created the runic alphabet, which had both practical and magical uses.

F	U	TH	A	R	K	H	N	I	A

S	T	B	M	L	R

RUNES

"Rune" comes from *runa*, meaning "secret" or "hidden." The runic alphabets (the shortened Scandinavian Fubark is shown here) are both a writing system and a set of magical symbols for divination. Runes were linked to the goddess Idun. Odin received knowledge of the runes by the sacrificial act of hanging himself on the Yggdrasil gallows tree for nine nights.

Examples of runic inscriptions of an everyday nature have been found, ranging from personal and business messages to bawdy and vulgar phrases. However, each letter was also thought to have mystical powers. They symbolized words, ideas, and concepts, with specific runes being associated with death, the sun, and the moon. Incised on sticks, bones, or stones, runes were drawn in groups of three and read for their meaning. They were also used in rituals for writing incantations, and as protective amulets and charms.

ANSUZ

Ansuz is the letter A and the fourth letter in the runic alphabet. It represents the mouth, messages, and the spoken word. In ancient oral traditions, the spoken word symbolized the vehicle of wisdom and knowledge. Ansuz can refer to advice or instruction received from a doctor, lawyer, teacher, or anyone who is more learned than the one questioning the runes. It can indicate an apprenticeship. In its reversed or negative aspect, it can mean receiving bad or biased advice. Combined with other negative runes, Ansuz can indicate the eternal student who never applies knowledge to life.

SOWILO

Sowilo is an S rune, meaning "sun." During the 1930s, the Nazis adopted the Sowilo rune (which in German is known as the *Sigrune*, or "victory rune"): two Sowilo runes were crossed to form the Nazi swastika and the SS used a double pair of Sowilo runes as their symbol. In the Norse tradition, the Sowilo rune stands for the sun, represents victory, and is associated with Baldr, the god of beauty and light. The Sowilo rune is also believed to bring honor and good luck to those who draw it in a reading.

THE AZTECS

The Aztecs achieved political and military dominance during the 14th, 15th, and 16th centuries, controlling large parts of Mesoamerica. The Aztec's main city, Tenochtitlan, was founded on the site of present-day Mexico City, where excavations have revealed their remarkable architectural and artistic accomplishments. The Aztecs had a mythological and religious tradition that included the worship of hundreds of deities and the practice of human sacrifice. They met their demise during the 16th century at the hands of the Spanish conquistadors, their population devastated by the diseases brought to the New World. Many contemporary Mexicans are descended from Aztec survivors and today more than one million Mexicans speak Nahuatl, the native Aztec language.

PACHAMAMA

Pachamama is a goddess revered to this day by Mesoamericans. Her name means "Mother Earth" or "Mother Universe," and she is a fertility goddess who presides over planting and harvesting. In some regions, people make offerings to her before gatherings by spilling a small amount of *chichi*, or beer, on the floor before drinking the rest. Pachamama's special worship day is called Martes de Challa, when people bury food in the earth and offer her candles and incense; this is celebrated one day before Ash Wednesday in the Christian calendar.

CORN

Maize or corn was a staple food of the ancient Mesoamericans and played a central part in their everyday lives. Flour made from corn provided dough for making flatbreads and the whole corn formed the main ingredient in daily meals. Understandably, corn gods and goddesses formed an important part of the Aztec pantheon. Chicomecoatl, the goddess of nourishment, who is depicted adorned with an elaborate tiered headdress, holds two pairs of ripe, tasseled cobs of corn in her extended hands. Her consort, the god Cinteotl, has yellow skin and maize in his hair. Another deity, the goddess Xilonen, the protector of young maize, is depicted as a virginal girl. (See also page 290.)

TRIPLE DEATH MASK

The passage of time was one of the main concerns in Aztec society and depictions of it captured their view of life. The Triple Death Mask represented the three phases of the human life cycle: birth and youth, maturity, and old age and death (the end of earthly life). Because these phases of life were believed to repeat, death was followed by lavish ceremonies and preparations for the next life. The Triple Death Mask was worn during religious and divinatory rites and was also used as a grave offering.

AZTEC CALENDAR

The famous Aztec calendar, or Sun Stone, was carved during the 15th century and is today recognized as a symbol of Mexico. The Aztecs dedicated this calendar to their sun god Tonatiuh, whose face appears at its center. Rings encircled his face, indicating different periods, days, and events in the natural and sacred worlds. Both numbers and symbols were used to record time. The Aztecs thought the whole universe was represented in the Sun Stone.

The calendar contained a 365-day civil calendar known as the Xiuhpohualli, which was linked to agriculture and the seasons, as well as a 260-day ritual or sacred calendar, known as the Tonalpolualli. The Xiuhpohualli divided the 365 days into 18 months of 20 days; the five days left over were used for festivities to mark the transition into the new year. The Tonalpolualli was divided into 20 periods of 13 days. Each day had a different symbol dedicated to a specific god. Some gods were considered positive and others negative, and would dictate the energy and mood of the day.

HEART

The Aztecs gave the energy of the heart and blood the name *teyolia*. It was this divine fire that animated humans, giving them their own unique identity. In return, it was thought that *teyolia* was necessary to strengthen, replenish, and sustain the gods. Toward this end, the Aztecs created the ritual of human sacrifice. Every 20 days, in a gruesome procedure, Aztec priests removed the beating hearts of their sacrificial victims, placed them in ritual bowls and offered them to the sun gods.

OLLIN

In the Nahuatl language of the Aztecs, *ollin* means "movement." Four Ollin glyphs frame the center of the Aztec calendar (Sun Stone) and together they represent the current epoch, which is named Earthquake Sun. The Aztecs believed that the world had been destroyed and recreated four times previously, and that the current epoch will succumb to an earthquake. They attempted to forestall the inevitable by appeasing the gods with rituals and sacrifice and with a steady diet of human blood.

DEATH EYE

In ancient times, life expectancy was short and death was a constant companion. The  "death eye"—which is represented as a straight line cutting through circles—is a common Aztec symbol found on many depictions of the gods. With a strong belief in an afterlife, the Aztecs felt that death was not something to be feared and that to die as a warrior or in a sacrificial rite was honorable. The highest level of paradise was Tonatiuhican, or the House of the Sun, where the souls of warriors and the victims of sacrifice resided.

SKULLS

Skulls are a frequent motif in Aztec art and often represent the skulls of sacrificial victims. Skull racks, or *tzompantli*, found near temples displayed hundreds of skulls —sometimes real and sometimes carved in stone—to commemorate sacrifices in honor of a god. They were also used as symbols of defeat and humiliation to intimidate subjugated populations. At the Great Temple of the Aztecs, archeologists found a skull rack with at least 240 carved skulls originally painted red.

The Aztec gods of death are often depicted with skull heads. Mictlantechtli has a skull head with large teeth and other deities are shown with skull heads and exposed ribs and bones. Skulls covered in jade (see page 323) were buried along with Aztec nobles, indicating the Aztec belief in an afterlife. The prevalence of skull imagery reflects the Aztec view of death as integral to life; their awareness and acceptance of death was a part of their everyday consciousness.

FEATHERED SERPENT

The cult of the serpent in Mesoamerica is very old. The feathered snake is said to have first appeared in Teotihuacan (not far from present-day Mexico City) around 150 BCE, as seen in the murals of the ancient city. Quetzalcoatl, the god of sky and earth, is depicted as a serpent covered in the bright-green feathers of the quetzal bird. As an archetype of the divine-human, the feathered serpent symbolizes the union of opposites: heaven and earth, male and female, matter and spirit. It also represents the incarnation of divine light into gross matter.

CAPTURED CITY

Among rival groups, the Aztecs participated in wars of conquest for the sole purpose of taking captives for human sacrifice to the gods. Captives from neighboring city-states were sacrificed to their sun god, Huitzilopochtli, whom they believed had chosen the Aztec nation above all others. Aztec warriors were in turn sacrificed to the reigning deity of whatever city captured them. The symbol of the captured city is a person being held by the hair; the name of the captured city is inscribed above the person's head.

THE MAYA

During their Classic Period from 250 to 900 CE, the Maya produced spectacular art and architecture as well as sophisticated mathematical and astronomical systems. Mayan symbols included many animal forms and a famous calendar. They also produced rich woven textiles decorated with symbols. A common motif was a diamond shape representing the universe and the path of the sun across the sky. Their mathematical system also involved the use of symbols— a dot represented one unit; a straight line, five units; and a shell, zero.

MAYAN CALENDAR

The Mayan calendar is a sophisticated system of 17 different synchronizing calendars. The two most important were the Haab, a 365-day calendar of 18 months of 20 days, based on the earth's rotation around the sun; and the Tzolkin, a 260-day calendar tied to the movement of the Pleiades constellation. The Tzolkin, made up of 13 cycles of 20 days, was used to time religious and ceremonial events and for divination. These two calendars together formed a 52-Haab cycle called the Calendar Round. The end of the Calendar Round provoked a period of great anxiety and unrest among the Maya, until they were sure the gods were going to grant them another cycle of 52 years.

Longer periods of time were tracked with the Long Count calendar, based on the mythological starting point of August 11, 3114 BCE. Skilled astronomers, the Maya created another calendar for tracking the planet Venus. This cycle was important for choosing auspicious times for coronations and war.

VISION SERPENT

The Vision Serpent is one of the most important of the Mayan serpent gods. During Mayan blood-letting rituals, participants would have a vision of a giant serpent that would permit them entrance to the spirit realm. They would then communicate with whatever the ancestor or god that emerged from the serpent's mouth. Thus, for the Maya, the Vision Serpent was the link between the spirit realm and the ordinary world.

THE SUN

The sun was highly regarded by Mayan civilization because it was thought to bring high crop yields and prosperity to the Mayan people. The sun was the symbol of royal authority and kings were referred to as Kinich Ahaw, or Sun-Eyed Lord. Kinich Kin, the sun god, was the patron of the city of Itzamal and was said to visit every day at noon. In Mayan script the Kin glyph means both "day" and "sun." The symbol for Kin, a day-blooming flower, was worn by Kinich Kin.

THE INCAS

The Incas thrived in South America from 1200 until 1533 CE, when the Spanish conquistador Francisco Pizarro killed the last emperor. The Incas believed they were descended from the sun and worshipped many gods and goddesses, including Pachamama and Pacha Camac—Earth Mother and Earth Father—and the sun god, Inti. For the Incas, the snake represented intellect, the puma courage, and the condor balance and life in another dimension. They believed that sacred sites, such as Machu Picchu, were places of power where spiritual energy was amplified.

INCA CALENDAR

Most experts agree that the Inca people developed calendars based on observation of the sun, moon, and stars. They used a solar calendar to choose optimal times for planting and harvesting. They also had names for 12 lunar months, although there is no evidence that they had a numerical system for counting time. The emperor god of the Incas, Viracocha, established the 12-month lunar year, with each month beginning with the new moon. His son, Pachacuti, built towers in order to observe the sun, so as to make adjustments to his father's calendar.

One of the primary functions of Machu Picchu, an ancient, secret ceremonial city built high in the Andes, was that of an astronomical observatory. The Inca observed the equinoxes there using shadow clocks such as the Intihuatana Stone, or Hitching Post of the Sun. The Intihuatana "hitches" the sun when, at midday on March 21 and September 21, the sun stands directly above the pillar, creating no shadow. Inca legends say that when someone touches his or her forehead to the Intihuatana, it opens that person's vision to the spirit world.

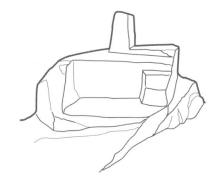

PUMA

The puma is associated with courage and internal strength. It is also connected with the theme of transition and the passage between this world and the underworld (Uku Pacha). The puma is thought to be a child of the earth and thus able to communicate with this realm. At the winter solstice, men dressed in puma skins initiated Inca boys into adult society. Thus the puma was associated with transitions in both the human and natural world. The name of Lake Titicaca means "meeting place of the pumas."

CONDOR

The condor, with its 10-foot (3-meter) wingspan, is the world's largest flying bird. The ancient Inca people associated it with Uku Pacha, the underworld, and with the inner worlds of birth, death, and fertility. Because it soared high in the sky, it was also identified with mountain peaks and was considered the keeper of lightning. The Inca identified the condor with the solar god Viracocha and worshipped it as a manifestation of the god himself. In Inca lore, the condor symbolizes living on after death in another dimension.

WESTERN AND MIDDLE EASTERN RELIGIONS

Many symbols rooted in Western and Middle Eastern religious traditions are found in contemporary art and culture. They are drawn from Judaism and the mystical Kabbalah, the many forms of Christianity, the esoteric traditions of Freemasonry, Gnosticism, and Rosicrucianism, contemporary forms of Wicca and witchcraft, and the ancient culture of Islam. Some symbols are shared, such as the star, which came to represent spiritual illumination and guidance to many traditions. For instance, in Christianity, the Star of Bethlehem guided the Magi to Christ's birthplace; in Islam, the star is a symbol of ascendancy and of God; and in Freemasonry, the blazing star is a symbol of divine providence.

JUDAISM AND THE KABBALAH

Judaism has existed for more than 4,000 years. It is a monotheistic religion (worshipping a single God) whose laws and beliefs stem from the covenant that God made with Abraham: the Jews would be God's chosen people if they followed the laws given to Moses. These laws were recorded in the Torah, the study of which is central to the Jewish faith. The Torah symbolizes the spiritual world and is housed in the Ark of Covenant, an ornate cabinet placed on the wall of the synagogue that faces the holy city of Jerusalem. The Kabbalah, the mystical arm of Judaism, outlines ten spheres, or Sephiroth, through which followers must pass in order to know God. The teachings of the Kabbalah were hidden to the uninitiated through a series of esoteric symbols.

MENORAH

The seven-branched menorah, or candelabrum, is one of the oldest symbols of the Jewish faith, found mostly in temples and synagogues. Ultimately its purpose is not to illuminate the temple, but to act as a physical reminder of Isaiah's commandment to be a light to the world. In the mystical tradition the light of the menorah is said to be drawn from *or ganuz*, the hidden residue of the original light of creation. The roots of the menorah symbol may lie in the ancient Babylonian World Tree or Tree of Life (see page 37).

STAR OF DAVID

The Star of David is also known as the Magen David, the Shield of David, and Solomon's Seal. The six-pointed Jewish star is a universally recognized symbol of Jewish identity and Judaism. Although its origin is unknown, Jewish legend says that the Star of David is modeled on the shield of King David, who unified ancient Israel. To save metal, he went into battle with a round shield made of leather stretched across two interlocking metal triangles. These two triangles symbolize male and female, the union of flesh and spirit, and active and passive principles. The six points of the Star of David plus the center give the number seven, which has religious significance in Judaism, referring to the six days of creation plus the seventh day of rest. The Star of David's structure of 3+3+1 also corresponds to the temple's menorah (see opposite), which was the more traditional symbol for Judaism in ancient times. In the Kabbalah, the Star of David symbolizes the six directions of space plus the center.

MEZUZAH

A mezuzah is a little scroll containing two short sections from the Torah, placed in a small metal, wooden, or ceramic case. It is affixed to the right-hand side of the door frame of Jewish homes to fulfil the biblical commandment to "inscribe the words of the Shema on the doorposts of your house"—the Shema being an affirmation of Judaism and the declaration of faith in one God. Qualified scribes prepare the parchment with indelible black ink and a special quill pen. As a talisman, the mezuzah symbolizes divine protection and draws God's blessings into the home.

TALLIS

In the Torah there is a commandment that Jews should wear tzitzit (strings) on the corners of their garments and so, during prayers, men wear the tallis, a large rectangular shawl fringed with tzitzit. The Talmud states that there are 248 positive and 365 negative commandments that Jews should observe. The sum of the mystical numbers equivalent to the letters that form the word tzitzit is 600; the five knots and eight threads of each fringe make up the other 13. By wrapping one's body in a tallis, one dedicates oneself totally to serving God.

TEFILLIN

Tefillin are leather pouches that are bound to arms and foreheads containing scrolls of Torah passages. At weekday morning services one case is tied to the arm, with the scrolls at the biceps and leather straps extending down the arm to the hand. Another case is tied to the head, with the case positioned on the forehead and the straps hanging down over the shoulders. Appropriate prayers and blessings are recited during this process. The tefillin are removed at the conclusion of the services. As with the mezuzah (see page 71), the scrolls must be handwritten.

CHAI

Chai (pronounced "hai") is a symbol and word that figures prominently in Jewish culture. It consists of the letters of the Hebrew alphabet Chet and Yud (see page 74), and means "living." According to the system of gematria (the numerology of the Hebrew language), the letters of Chai add up to 18. For this reason 18 is a lucky number in Judaism and many Jews give gifts of money in multiples of 18. For both men and women, the Chai symbol is worn as a medallion around the neck.

TETRAGRAMMATON

YHWH (Yahweh), the sacred name of God in Jewish scriptures, is also known as the Tetragrammaton. Because Hebrew was written without vowels in ancient times, God's name was represented by the four consonants Y, H, W, H. The letters may be derived from the Hebrew verb "to be," emphasizing God's absolute being, without beginning or end. The Tetragrammaton was inscribed on the rod of Aaron and the ring of Solomon. In the Kabbalah, it symbolizes mystical power.

UNIVERSAL ALPHABET

For Kabbalists, the 22 letters of the Hebrew alphabet, the Aleph-Beit, transcend religion, geography, and race, and are themselves universal instruments of power. The Hebrew word for "letter" translates as "pulse" or "vibration." Each letter in the Aleph-Beit is considered a manifestation of the energy of the universe and an ancient key for unlocking the mysteries of the spiritual world.

According to the earliest known book on Jewish mysticism, the *Sefer Yetzirah* (*Book of Creation*), God created the universe in the form of Sephiroth, the ten sacred numbers. Then the second set of Sephiroth appeared, the 22 letters of the Hebrew alphabet. Kabbalists believe that these letters, brought together in different combinations, gave rise to both words and matter, creating language and the universe at the same time. Drawing on the divine power residing in the letters, Kabbalists meditate on their forms as portals to sacred truths and to their own souls. Contemplating various combinations of letters releases emotions and brings spiritual realization, positive change, and healing into the initiate's life.

ALEPH	BET	GIMMEL	DALED	HAY	VAV	ZAYIN	CHET
YET	YUD	KAF	LAMED	MEM	WUN	SAMECH	AYIN
PAY	TSADEE	KIF	RESH	SHIN	TAF		

SEPHIROTHIC TREE

The Sephirothic Tree of Life (see also page 37) represents the central system of Jewish Kabbalistic thought. This arrangement of ten interconnected spheres, or Sephiroth, represents the attributes that God created, through which he manifests the physical and mystical universe. Together, the ten Sephiroth provide a step-by-step blueprint of creation and the individual's path to enlightenment. None of the ten Sephiroth are separate from the others; they function in a mystical state of unity within the Tree of Life, forming a more complete view of the perfected whole.

The ten Sephiroth are divided into four realms: Atziluth, the world of the supernatural; Beriah, the creative world of archetypes and ideals; Yetsirah, the world of formation; and Assiah, the material world of manifest creation. The Sephiroth are connected by 22 channels or paths, representing the 22 letters of the Hebrew alphabet. When combined with the ten Sephiroth, the 22 paths give the number 32, which refers to the 32 Kabbalistic Paths of Wisdom. These 32 paths derive from the first 32 verses of Genesis, in which the Name of God (Elohim) is mentioned 32 times.

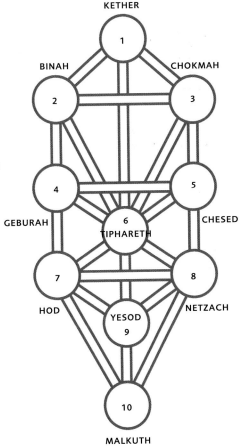

CHRISTIANITY

Christianity, one of the oldest and most widespread religions, finds expression in a profusion of symbols that are commonly found in Western art and architecture. From earliest times, Christian symbolism was used to teach Church doctrine in order to make the concepts easier to grasp and memorize in what was a basically illiterate society. Consequently, Christian symbols abound in medieval and Renaissance art, most notably in the rose windows and wall murals of European cathedrals. Common symbols include the halo, which indicates the sacredness of the person whose head it surrounds, and the cross, the universal emblem of Christianity.

LATIN CROSS

The Latin cross, the *crux immissa*, is the simplest and most common form of the cross. The vertical trunk extends above the transverse beam, which is set two-thirds of the way up the trunk. In Catholic settings, a crucifix with Jesus on the cross is more common, whereas Protestants prefer the empty cross, symbolizing the resurrection. Many medieval churches were designed in the form of the Latin cross, with the vertical trunk of the cross forming the nave, thus creating a symbolic reference to the cross of Christ.

GREEK CROSS

A very early form of the Christian cross, the Greek cross or *crux quadrata*, predates the Latin cross (see opposite). It has arms of equal length and its pre-Christian origins date back to ancient Babylon, where it was a symbol of the sun god Shamash. In Christianity, the Greek cross does not represent the Crucifixion but rather symbolizes the four directions of the earth, the spread of the Gospel in four directions, and the four Evangelists. A Greek cross within a square represents the temporal authority of the Church.

INVERTED CROSS

The inverted cross is known as the Cross of St. Peter. According to Catholic tradition, St. Peter was crucified upside down because he did not feel worthy to be crucified in the same position as Christ. As popes are considered the successors of St. Peter, the inverted cross became a symbol of the papacy and is found on papal thrones and tombs. It is often combined with two keys, symbolizing the keys to the kingdom of heaven that were promised to St. Peter (see page 164). The keys also symbolize the Pope's authority.

CROSS OF CALVARY

The cross of Calvary is a Latin cross (see page 76) mounted on three steps. These steps symbolize the Hill of Calvary, the hill outside Jerusalem's gate on which Christ was crucified, and the Via Dolorosa, the road along which Christ carried the cross to his death. In descending order, the steps are said to symbolize the three theological virtues of faith, hope, and charity. The design is commonly used for gravestones and is then referred to as a stepped cross. The Calvary cross is sometimes adorned with a cloth, or shroud, draped over the crossbeam.

STAR

In the Christian tradition, a star shining in the dark symbolizes the soul's struggle for redemption. It signifies that divine guidance and wisdom come from the heavens rather than the earthly realms. The Bible refers to Christ as the "Morning Star." The Star of Bethlehem revealed the birth of Jesus to the Magi and later guided them to Bethlehem. The Marian star (the symmetric six-pointed star) is associated with the Virgin Mary; in her form as Queen of Heaven, Mary is depicted wearing a crown of 12 stars, which symbolize the 12 apostles.

THE TRIUMPHANT CROSS

This cross atop an orb (see page 167), symbolizing Christ's triumph over the world, is found in images of Christ as *Salvator Mundi*, or Savior of the World. Before Christianity, pagan rulers would hold an orb to symbolize their temporal power over all creation. Christian rulers added a cross, to show Christ's dominion over the world and Christianity's triumph over paganism.

ICTHTHYS/ICHTHUS

Ichthys is the classical Greek word for "fish." It is an acronym, based on the initial Greek letters of "Jesus Christ, Son of God" or *Iesous Christos, Theou Yios Soter*. Early Christians used the *ichthys* sign, consisting of two intersecting arcs resembling the profile of a fish, as a secret symbol and it marked graves in the catacombs where persecuted Christians would meet in secret. At the time a similar symbol was used by Greeks to mark the location of funerals, giving Christians a legitimate reason to gather.

Fish are mentioned and given symbolic meaning several times in the Gospels. Several of the 12 disciples of Jesus were fishermen and he referred to them as "fishers of men." At the feeding of the five thousand, Jesus multiplied five loaves and two fish. Jesus compared God's decision about who will go to heaven or hell at the end of this world to fishers sorting out their catch, keeping the good fish and throwing away the bad. Early Christian fathers called their followers of Christ *pisculi*, or fish.

HOLY CHALICE

The Holy Chalice is said to be the vessel that Jesus used at the Last Supper. According to one Christian legend, St. Peter used the Holy Chalice to say Mass. After Peter's death, the cup was passed on to successor popes, until Sixtus II in 258 CE, when the Roman emperor Valerian demanded possession of all relics. In defiance, Sixtus gave the Holy Chalice to St. Lawrence, who safeguarded it at his home in Spain. It was then passed to a series of Spanish monarchs, up to King Alfonso in 1200. During his reign the relic reverted to the Spanish Church.

In an entirely different and conflicting story, the cup of the Last Supper is known as the Holy Grail. In this legend, the cup was used to collect and store the blood of Christ at the Crucifixion.

In Catholic theology, the wine that is consecrated in the Mass becomes the true blood of Christ. In both of these stories the Holy Chalice or Holy Grail is a cup that holds the blood of Jesus Christ, either in sacramental or literal form.

AGNUS DEI/LAMB OF GOD

Lamb of God, or *Agnus Dei*, is one of the names given to Jesus in the New Testament and used in the Christian tradition to refer to the role of Jesus as a sacrificial lamb atoning for the sins of the world. The idea of the Lamb of God may have its origin in ancient sacrifices that were conducted during Passover at the Jewish Temple, in which a pure, unblemished lamb was sacrificed, its blood poured out and offered as atonement for sins. In the same way, Christians believe that they can be freed from sin by the blood of Jesus, as the unblemished Lamb of God.

A litany beginning with the words "Lamb of God" is used in the Roman Catholic Mass: *Agnus Dei, qui tollis peccata mundi, miserere nobis . . .* ("O Lamb of God, who takes away the sins of the world, have mercy upon us . . .")

The Lamb of God is a symbol of purity, innocence, and renewal. It is depicted with a halo and a banner with a red cross on a white background, symbolizing resurrection. (See also page 237.)

DOVE

In the Christian tradition, the dove stands for purity, simplicity, redemption, and peace. A dove symbolizes the Holy Spirit, one of three manifestations of the Holy Trinity (see opposite), along with God the Father and God the Son (Jesus Christ). As a symbol of the Holy Spirit, the dove appears in representations of the baptism of Christ, signifying his divinity. A dove made of gold was hung in the baptistery at Reims in France after the baptism of Clovis, who ruled France during the 5th century CE. When identified with martyrdom, the dove indicated the Holy Spirit's bestowal of fortitude necessary to bear the suffering. The dove is also a symbol of the Church, as the vehicle though which the Holy Spirit works on earth.

On a sarcophagus or other funeral monuments, a representation of the dove bearing an olive branch signifies the peace of the departed soul or the hope of resurrection. This symbolism is derived from the story of Noah and the Flood, in which a dove brought back an olive branch, informing Noah that the Flood was over. (See also page 258.)

TRINITY

The Holy Trinity, a central dogma of Christian theology, states that God is one being who exists, simultaneously and eternally, as a mutual indwelling of three persons: the Father, the Son (Jesus Christ), and the Holy Spirit. Belief in the Trinity is accepted among all forms of Catholic and mainstream Protestant traditions. The concept of the Holy Trinity was expressed in early writings from the beginning of the 2nd century CE on.

Tertullian, a Roman theologian who wrote in the early 3rd century, was the first to use the words "Trinity," "person," and "substance" to explain that the Father, Son, and Holy Spirit are "one in essence—not one in Person." About a century later the First Council of Nicaea in 325 CE confirmed the doctrine of the Trinity and formulated the Nicene Creed that described Christ as "begotten, not made" and of "one substance with the Father."

The triquetra, which is made up of three interlocking arcs, is a pagan symbol adopted by Christians to represent the concepts of the Trinity and eternity.

ALPHA AND OMEGA

The term Alpha and Omega is used to describe God in the Book of Revelation. It is the first and last letters of the classical Greek alphabet (see page 352), or A and Z. Most Christian denominations apply the name to Christ as well as God, the letters suggesting that Christ is "the First and the Last" or "the Beginning and the End." In other words, this symbol stands for the belief that Jesus existed from the dawn of time and will exist for all eternity.

CHI RHO

Chi Rho (pronounced "ki row") is probably the oldest symbol for the name of Christ. It was found inscribed along the walls of Roman catacombs, the cemeteries of the early Christians. Chi and Rho are the first two letters in the Greek word for Christ. Chi is shaped like an X, while Rho has the shape of the letter P (see page 352). Overlaying Rho and Chi produces the "XP" of the Chi Rho symbol. This is the origin of the practice of abbreviating "Christmas" to "Xmas."

SACRED HEART

The Sacred Heart is a symbol of the physical heart of Jesus and of his divine love for humanity. It is depicted in Christian art as a flaming heart glowing with divine light, pierced by a lance wound, wrapped in a crown of thorns, and bleeding. The wounds and crown of thorns symbolize the Crucifixion of Christ and his sacrifice for humankind, while the surrounding fire represents the transformative power of love. Devotion to the Sacred Heart is predominant in the Roman Catholic Church.

IHS

IHS is an abbreviation for IHESUS, which is the medieval spelling of "Jesus" and consists of the Greek letters Iota, Eta, and Sigma (see page 352). St. Ignatius of Loyola adopted the IHS monogram as the seal for the Society of Jesus, or Jesuit Order. Today, IHS usually symbolizes the communion wafer. The solar rays depicted surrounding the emblem represent the monstrance, a decorated vessel used to display the communion host. The solar symbolism may refer to earlier use of Roman ritual implements.

FREEMASONRY

William Schaw, who was made King James VI of Scotland's Master of Works in 1583, was the founder of modern Freemasonry. Stonemasons who were introduced into the brotherhood were given their mason's mark and were taught the art of building, along with Christian morals and ethics. By the 18th century, Freemasonry included more non-masons than masons and no longer functioned as a true craftsmen's guild, but rather as a fraternal organization dedicated to personal and spiritual development.

MASON'S MARK

When stonemasons organized into guilds in the 14th century, they began using unique marks or symbols to identify their work on stone buildings and other public structures. When an apprentice stonemason became a journeyman, he would choose a mark that was his to use for life. The mark was given at a solemn ceremony that was presided over by master stonemasons and concluded with the mark being entered in a record book.

There were two types of marks used by stonemasons: laying-out marks, which were applied at the quarry to expedite construction on site, and signature marks that identified a particular mason. The signature mark is what is generally meant by the term "mason's mark." This not only identified the mason in question, but also attested to his character, integrity,

reputation, and skill. It may have had a practical purpose as a means to claim payment for work completed.

Some special marks may have been used by medieval Freemasons to show that secret principles of geometry were used in the building of a church.

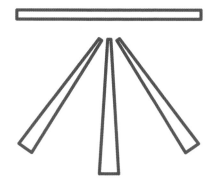

SET SQUARE AND COMPASS

The best-known symbol associated with Freemasonry is the overlapping compass and set square with a letter G in the center. Since Freemasonry considers itself flexible, there is no definitive interpretation for the meaning of the set square and compass symbol. However, modern Freemasons suggest that these instruments symbolize a variety of positive virtues, including craft, skill, judgment, and discernment.

The compass represents the restraint of excess passions and negative emotions, which are circumscribed or controlled by the feminine compass. The right angle of the set square measures the square, a masculine symbol of the earth and the material world. The square also symbolizes fairness, balance, and firmness (see also page 372). Something squared is thought to be stable, in alignment with morals and ethics, and suitable as a foundation for building upon. The letter G in the center is said to refer either to geometry or to God, who is regarded as the Grand Architect of the universe. Some say that the three elements of the Freemasonry symbol refer to the three degrees of Masonry: the Apprentice Degree, Fellow Craft Degree, and Master Mason Degree.

BLAZING STAR

The Freemasons' five-pointed star finds its source in the pentagram of Pythagoras. Encoded into the pentagram's structure is the golden ratio (see page 378), a unique proportion in geometry said to embody divine beauty in form. Masons used the golden ratio extensively in the design and construction of early cathedrals. For contemporary Freemasons the five-pointed star, or blazing star, is a symbol of light and the mystic center of the universe. It represents the effort of perfecting the self, with the motivation of illuminating a dark and unconscious world.

EYE IN A TRIANGLE

The eye in a triangle, sometimes referred to as the eye of Providence or the all-seeing eye, is found in Masonic texts and rituals. It symbolizes spiritual knowledge and reminds the lodge member that the Grand Architect of the universe is always judging his words and deeds. The Eye of Providence was a common symbol in the 17th and 18th centuries, when Masonic ritual and symbolism was evolving. It is not surprising that many symbols common to general society made their way into Masonic ceremonies.

BLAZING SUN

Masonic symbols are found as decorative features on many older buildings. The set square and compass (see page 87) are very common, as is the blazing sun—a symbol of the light of God, the universe, and eternity. It also represents the journey of the initiate through each of the three principal stations of the Masonic lodge. The face in the blazing sun represents the face of God, as well as the face of the Masonic master.

OUROBOROS

The ouroboros, meaning "tail devourer," is an ancient symbol depicting a serpent swallowing its own tail and forming a circle (see also page 271). It may have been inspired by the night sky, as some ancient texts refer to a serpent of light residing in the heavens. It is a symbol found in many cultures and generally represents concepts of circularity, unity, or infinity. As a Masonic symbol, the ouroboros represents eternity, renewal, love, and wisdom. Like the set square and compass (see page 87), it is used as an architectural decoration on building facades and is incorporated into floors and ceilings.

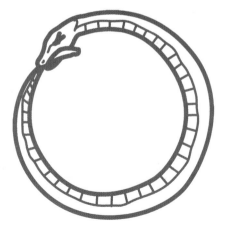

IMMOVABLE JEWELS

In the American system of Freemasonry, the Immovable Jewels are the square, level, and plumb. They are named "immovable" because they are placed in fixed positions in the lodge—the square to the east, the level to the west, and the plumb to the south. The three principal officers of the lodge who sit in these positions wear replicas of the tools.

The square, level, and plumb are important and valuable tools for the builder, for without them he cannot work. For the Freemason, these tools symbolize the building of the moral self. The plumb line is a symbol of right, uprightness, and proper social and moral behavior; a Mason is expected to lead an upright life and be of value to his fellow men. The square represents virtue, telling the truth, and dealing honestly with others. The level is a symbol of equality and of the need to treat all men with respect, dignity, and understanding.

In the British system the Immovable Jewels are the rough ashlar, the perfect ashlar, and the tracing board. The rough ashlar is an unhewn block of stone symbolizing man in his natural, untutored state, with all his faults and potential for improvement. The perfect ashlar is the educated man, refined and with his mind illuminated or filled with light. The tracing board is a chart of emblems used for illustrating the lectures.

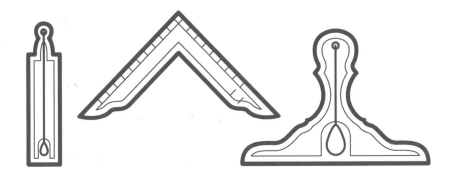

WINDING STAIRS

The image of winding stairs represents the winding stairs of life that a Mason climbs steadily, from birth to his final resting place. It is a symbol of the Masonic process of inner growth and the building of character. The stairs wind to represent the mystery or secret aspects of life's journey. A winding staircase is unpredictable and hides from view that which is around the corner, so it takes courage, faith, and determination to continue the climb.

According to Masons, the steps of the winding staircase began at the entrance of the Temple. The world of the profane was without the Temple; the world of the initiated was within its sacred walls. Symbolically, during the Fellow Craft Degree, the initiate advances into the sanctuary, where he finds the winding stair that invites him to ascend. This is the symbol of the Masonic labor of personal self-improvement and character development, and of discipline, research, and instruction—the end of which is to be the possession of divine truth.

GNOSTICISM

The term "Gnostic" comes from the Greek word *gnosis*, meaning "knowledge." The Gnostic gospels, now called the Nag Hammadi Library, were discovered in Egypt in 1945. Gnostic philosophy may have originated in pre-Christian times or may have been contemporaneous with Christ himself. Gnostics believed that Christ was not a human being, but rather an avatar or a manifestation in the guise of a human being. In Gnosticism, the serpent is a symbol of awakening to higher consciousness.

ABRACADABRA

The word "abracadabra," known today as the "magic word" of stage magicians, is an ancient word that appeared in Kabbalistic and Gnostic texts. As both a magical incantation and a talisman, it invoked the aid of beneficent spirits against disease and misfortune. It was written as an inverted pyramid, with the entire word at the top and one fewer letter in each line, until only the letter A remained. The command to the fever or evil spirit was to "perish like these words." By gradually reducing the number of letters in the incantation or charm, the evil spirit was eased out of its victim and was itself reduced to nothing.

The Gnostic physician Serenus Sammonicus, who lived during the 2nd to 3rd centuries CE, prescribed abracadabra as a remedy for curing fevers and gave precise instructions concerning its use. It was to be written on paper, then folded and worn for nine days as an amulet. Before sunrise of the tenth day it was to be cast behind the wearer into a stream flowing to the east.

```
A B R A C A D A B R A
 A B R A C A D A B R
  A B R A C A D A B
   A B R A C A D A
    A B R A C A D
     A B R A C A
      A B R A C
       A B R A
        A B R
         A B
          A
```

ABRAXAS

Abraxas, a name known from the Gnostic writings of Simon Magus (a pre-Christian religious teacher, magician, philosopher, and contemporary of the Apostles, supposedly the founder of the Simonian sect of Gnosticism), is said to be a replacement for the unmentionable name of the Supreme Being. According to the Gnostic scholar Basilides (early 2nd century CE), the word "Abraxas" is created using the first letters of the names of the seven visible planets. Gematrically—that is, using the numerical value of Hebrew letters—the letters in Abraxas add up to 365, the number of days in a solar year and the number of aeons, or divine emanations, in Gnostic cosmology. Each of the seven letters represents one of the seven planetary powers.

The image most associated with Abraxas is that of a composite creature with the head of a rooster, the body of a man, and the legs of a serpent. He is depicted carrying a whip, which symbolizes wisdom, and a shield, which symbolizes power. Amulets and seals bearing the figure of Abraxas were common in the 2nd century CE, and during the 13th century the figure of Abraxas was found in the seals of the Knights Templar. However, by medieval times Abraxas was relegated to the rank of a demon.

ROSICRUCIANISM

A pamphlet supposedly written by the mythical knight Christian Rosenkreuz in 1614 was the spur to the creation of the Rosicrucian secret society. The Rosy Cross was used to symbolize the blood that Christ lost on the cross, and the seven levels of initiation were represented by the seven petals that formed the flower. The modern worldwide Rosicrucian Order, which was founded in the United States in 1915 by Harvey Spencer Lewis, promotes mystical, educational, and humanitarian values without allegiance to any religion.

ROSICRUCIAN ROSE

The Rosicrucian rose is illustrated in the same way as the rose depicted in the center of early compasses. The compasses showed the four principal winds and later the four cardinal directions in the shape of a cross: north, south, east, and west. Rosicrucians considered themselves Rose Cross men—those who used a metaphoric rose compass to embark on a voyage to gather knowledge from all parts of the world, in pursuit of illumination and personal growth.

The rose on the emblem of the Rosicrucians may also refer to Martin Luther's rose and cross emblem, because many early Rosicrucians were Lutherans. Later the Christian connotations of the Rosicrucian rose became stronger, symbolizing the gradual unfolding of spiritual realization and the triumph of spirit over matter. The red color of the rose represents the blood of Christ and the golden heart at the center of the flower corresponds to the spiritual gold hiding within human nature. The rose itself symbolizes the heart, a Christian emblem of the virtues of love and compassion.

CRUCIFIED ROSE

The "jewel" of the Rosicrucian fraternity is a symbol of a rose in the center of a Calvary cross raised on three steps (see page 78). The cross may be depicted as made of transparent red stone, with a red cross on one side and a red rose on the other. The crucified rose has several meanings, including the human soul crucified on the cross of the material plane, and the stages of initiation, with the center symbolizing unity with Christ.

GOLDEN CROSS/ROSY CROSS

Worn as an insignia by Rosicrucians, the equal-armed gold cross is properly referred to as the Rosy Cross. It often bears alchemical symbols and inscriptions such as "faith," "hope," "love," and "patience." It stands for the transcendental and transformational process of the Rosicrucian movement and its effort to establish itself as a force of Light in the material world. It also signifies the initiate's process of transmuting ignorance into the pure gold of wisdom through rituals and learning the secrets of the brotherhood, thus achieving a more evolved state.

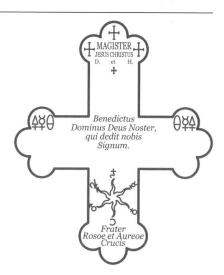

WICCA AND WITCHCRAFT

Witchcraft is the practice of using magical powers and supernatural forces for sorcery and divination. Witches are said to have the power to fly, to change shape, and to cast spells for good or harm. Wiccans are neo-pagans who are involved in the positive exploration of Wicca (a nature-based religion) or witchcraft in modern times. Modern Wicca precludes the hurting of others and derives power from psychological and psychosomatic effects, rather than from attempts at paranormal or supernatural interventions. Wiccans use personal spells or those handed down from other practitioners.

WITCHES' PENTANGLE

A symbol of witchcraft, the pentangle is a pentagram (or five-pointed star) within a circle. The five points of the pentagram represent the four elements or four directions, with the uppermost point representing the sanctity of Spirit. The pentangle is used in the Wiccan practice of summoning the elemental spirits of the four directions at the beginning of a ritual. Pentangles are also the suit of earth in the Tarot deck.

The outer circle of the circumscribed pentagram is sometimes interpreted as binding the elements together or bringing them into harmony with each other. The pentangle is also associated with the quest for divine knowledge.

WAND

Wiccan practitioners use wands for channeling energy, healing, and the casting of spells. Though traditionally made of wood, wands can also be made of metal or crystal. Most practitioners cut a branch from a tree and use it in its natural form, or they may carve and decorate it in order to personalize it. In Wicca, the wand usually represents the element of fire. The wand may have its roots in the drumstick used in ceremonies by tribal shamans or medicine-priests.

ATHAME

The athame is the ritual knife of witchcraft ceremonies, representing the fire element and the masculine qualities of consciousness, force, and action. It often has a double-edged blade, with a black handle that may be inscribed with Wiccan symbols. The athame is used to direct energy and may be employed to cast the magical circle—a circle or sphere marked out during rituals to contain energy, create sacred space, or provide protection. When the ritual or ceremony has ended, the practitioner closes the circle by drawing it counterclockwise with the athame.

CHALICE

The chalice is a symbol of the element of water and of the feminine. A chalice represents intuition, psychic ability, and the subconscious. It also symbolizes the Goddess, the womb, and the female generative organs. It is often used in rituals along with the athame, the symbol of the male principle. The chalice and the blade together symbolize sexual union. The ceremonial use of the chalice is as the holder of ritual liquid, whether this is water to purify the circle or wine for a feast or ritual libation.

HIDDEN PENTANGLE

Hidden pentangles—pentangles disguised in intricate designs—can be worn when it is not safe or appropriate to wear a standard witchcraft pentangle (see page 96). They are sometimes called flower pentangles. These stylized designs can be recognized by other practitioners of the Craft, but are less apparent to others and so less likely to cause problems with a non-pagan family or in the workplace. Wearing a pentangle in any form acts as a protective amulet.

ELEVEN STAR

The eleven star (also called the fairy star) is a seven-pointed star associated with practitioners of the Celtic fairy traditions of Wicca. Fairy Wiccans focus on gnomes, fairies and sprites and their relation to the natural world. The eleven star is used interchangeably with the pentagram. The seven points represent the seven directions: the four cardinal directions (north, south, east, and west) plus above, below, and within. They can also represent the seven magical elements: the four alchemical elements (fire, earth, air, and water) plus magic, light, and life; or seven magical places: the sun, moon, sea, sky, wood, wind, and spirit.

DEGREES OF INITIATION

In Wicca, a degree system of initiation marks the candidate's level of understanding and proficiency in the Craft. The symbols that accompany each degree represent a special salute in which the hand touches parts of the body in an uninterrupted motion.

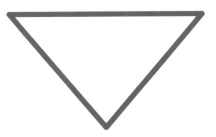

FIRST DEGREE

The first degree inducts the witch into the coven and introduces the basic teachings and traditions. The inverted triangle symbolizes the salute: breast, genitals, and return to the breast.

SECOND DEGREE (I)

The second degree has two levels. The first part acknowledges progress made following induction and its symbol is an upward-pointing triangle to match the salute: mouth, breast, breast, mouth.

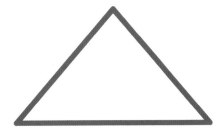

SECOND DEGREE (II)

A down-pointing pentagram represents the second level of the second degree for candidates who have further deepened their knowledge of the rituals and skills. The order of the salute follows the pentagram: genitals, right breast, left hip, right hip, left breast, genitals.

THIRD DEGREE

The third degree is granted to witches who have shown the highest proficiency. The symbol is an upright triangle atop an upright pentangle. The salute is mouth, breast, breast, mouth, genitals, right foot, left knee, right knee, left foot, genitals.

BOOK OF SHADOWS

A book of shadows is a collection of magical and religious texts of Wicca and other witchcraft traditions, containing their core rituals, magical practices, ethics, and philosophy. In traditional Wicca, it is copied by hand from the book of one's initiating high priestess or priest, who in turn copied theirs from their initiator. The original book of shadows was put together by Gerald Gardner (1884–1964), who first popularized Wicca. Gardner's book began as a personal journal, but later became a religious text that was used in most traditions of Wicca.

In contemporary Wiccan practice, the term "book of shadows" normally describes a witch's personal journal, rather than a traditional text. It is a witch's collection of rituals, spells, recipes, and other magical information. This text is not normally passed from teacher to student. In some cases the contemporary book of shadows is an electronic document residing on a computer or a website. Some Wiccans reserve their book of shadows for recording spells and magical information and keep a separate book, sometimes called the book of mirrors, for personal thoughts, feelings, and experiences.

EARTH

AIR

FIRE

WATER

HORNED GOD

The Horned God is the main god that is worshipped in Wicca. He is a composite of horned male nature gods from various traditions, such as the Celtic Cernunnos (see page 54), the English Herne the Hunter, the Egyptian Osiris, the Greek Pan, and the Roman Faunus. As such, the Horned God functions as a universal masculine archetype. He is sometimes referred to as the Great God, who impregnates the Goddess in the autumn and then dies, only to be reborn in spring.

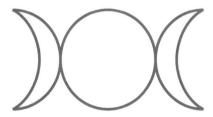

TRIPLE GODDESS

The Triple Goddess, the Horned God's female counterpart, is depicted in several ways. In one of the best-known Wiccan symbols she is represented as the three phases of the moon—a circle or full moon with a crescent moon on each side—but sometimes she is shown as three crescent moons intertwined with each other. The three phases of the moon represent the three stages of a woman's life: maiden, mother, and crone. As a goddess, the Triple Goddess is the Wiccan archetype for the feminine aspect of the universe. (See also pages 46, 52, and 118.)

ISLAM

Islam is a monotheistic, Abrahamic religion founded in the seventh century by the Prophet Muhammad (570–632 CE), the Arab religious and political leader. The word "Islam" means "submission," referring to the total surrender of oneself to God. A follower of Islam is known as a Muslim, meaning "one who submits to God." The Five Pillars of Islam are the five beliefs of Muslims: belief in Allah and the teachings of the prophet Muhammad (Shahadah); ritual prayer five times a day (Salat); alms-giving (Zakat); fasting (Ramadan); and pilgrimage to Mecca at least once in a lifetime (Hajj). Islam prohibits the realistic depiction of the human form or nature for the purpose of worship and so elements such as calligraphy and the arabesque became important vehicles of expression and symbolism throughout the Islamic world.

ARABESQUE

The arabesque, an element of Islamic art, is an elaborate repeating geometric form that is often found as a decorative motif on the walls of mosques. To Muslims, the arabesque creates a meditative rhythm that extends beyond the visible material world and the constraints of time. It symbolizes the infinite, the pervasive, and the all-encompassing nature of creation, which is the expression of the one God, Allah. The arabesque form represents spirituality without the use of iconography, which is forbidden in Islam.

STAR AND CRESCENT

Because Diana was the patron goddess of Byzantium, the city's symbol was a crescent moon. In 330 CE the emperor Constantine rededicated the city—which he called Constantinople—to the Virgin Mary and superimposed the star symbol over the crescent. In 1453 Constantinople was captured by the Islamic Ottoman Turks and renamed Istanbul, but its new rulers adopted the existing emblem for their own use. Today the star and crescent feature on the flags and coins of Islamic countries, with the crescent representing divine authority and the star, paradise.

ZULFIQAR

One of the best-known symbols in Islam, Zulfiqar, or Muhammad's sword, is especially important to Shi'a Muslims. Muhammad passed on Zulfiqar to his son-in-law and cousin, Ali ibn Abi Talib (c.599–661 CE), a famous warrior from Medina, who used it against a fierce adversary from Mecca at the Battle of Uhud in 625 CE. Muhammad is reported to have said, "There is no hero but Ali, and no sword except Zulfiqar," a phrase that is still widely engraved on Muslim weapons today. Zulfiqar also symbolizes the sharp distinction between right and wrong.

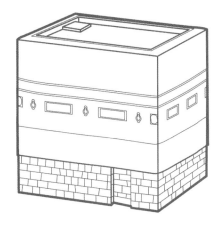

KAABA

The Kaaba, a masonry structure in the shape of a cube located within the Great Mosque at Mecca, is the most important shrine in Islam. It is around the Kaaba that ritual circumambulation is performed by Muslims during the Hajj pilgrimage. A black silk cloth decorated with gold embroidered passages from the Koran, known as the Kiswah, is used to cover the Kaaba and prevents anyone from looking directly at the Kaaba, which is forbidden.

The Kaaba predated Islam and was originally used to worship various Arabian tribal gods. In the 7th century Muhammad preached the religion of Islam and claimed the shrine for the worship of God (Allah) alone. The tribe resisted and ousted Muhammad and his followers. In 630 he returned to Mecca, conquered the tribe and rededicated the Kaaba as an Islamic house of worship. Henceforth the annual pilgrimage to Mecca, known as the Hajj, became a Muslim rite.

In the eastern corner of the Kaaba is the sacred Black Stone, thought to be a meteorite remnant. The stone symbolizes divine power and direct communication between God and humans.

HAND OF FATIMA

This is a symbol of power, strength, and protection. The upraised hand symbolizes the five pillars of Islam: faith, prayer, pilgrimage, fasting, and charity. The name refers to Fatima Zahra (606/615–632), daughter of Muhammad. For Shi'a Muslims, Fatima has the same stature as the Virgin Mary does for Catholics and is considered holy and without sin. As a model for Muslim women, she is known as Mistress of the Women of the World. The hand of Fatima is worn as an amulet for protection (see page 334).

ISLAMIC COLOR SYMBOLISM

A symbol of Islam, the color green (see page 388) is used for the bindings of the Koran. Muhammad wore a green cloak and turban and Muslim warriors wore green in the Crusades. Green represents life, nature, and fertility. Green and gold are the colors of paradise. The Koran says that those who reach paradise will wear green silk robes and recline on green cushions.

Black (see page 391) is a talisman against the evil eye. It is the color of sadness and sorrow. Black is also the color of the chador (the cloak worn by devout Muslim women) and of the cloaks worn by Shi'ite clergy. White (see page 391) is a positive

color and symbolizes purity and peace. It is the color of angels, of the shroud used to cover bodies of the deceased, and of a student's long tunic. Many Muslims wear white when attending Friday prayers.

EASTERN RELIGIONS

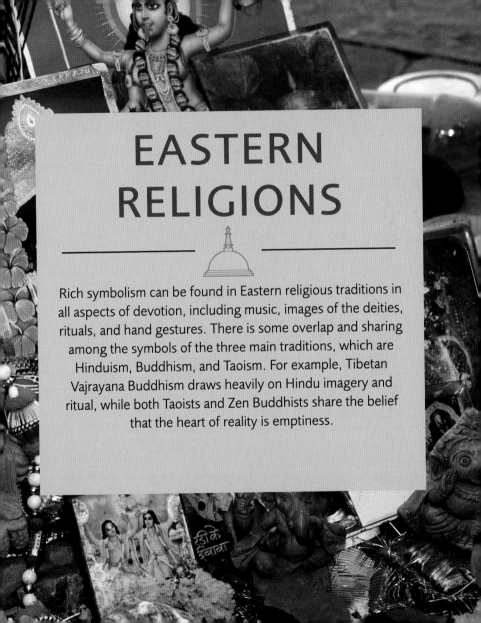

Rich symbolism can be found in Eastern religious traditions in all aspects of devotion, including music, images of the deities, rituals, and hand gestures. There is some overlap and sharing among the symbols of the three main traditions, which are Hinduism, Buddhism, and Taoism. For example, Tibetan Vajrayana Buddhism draws heavily on Hindu imagery and ritual, while both Taoists and Zen Buddhists share the belief that the heart of reality is emptiness.

HINDUISM

Hinduism, which developed from the earlier Vedic religion, is the oldest living Eastern tradition. The Vedas—the holy scriptures of Hinduism—provide information about Hindu religious thought, including reincarnation and karma, and include songs and rituals for worshipping the many Hindu deities who are manifestations of the Supreme Cosmic Spirit, Brahman. Each of the major and minor Hindu deities has special symbols associated with them and every object that is used in rituals and ceremonial offerings has symbolic significance.

PURNAKUMBHA

The *purnakumbha* is a brass, mud, or copper pot used for religious ceremonies. Mango leaves are placed at the mouth of the pot and a red thread is tied around its neck and sometimes covers the pot in an intricate design. The pot is then filled with water, which symbolizes the divine life force, Mother Earth, and the primordial water from which all life emerged. The thread represents the love that binds all creation. The *purnakumbha* is used at the start of a puja (ritual worship performed by most Hindus on a daily basis) and is offered to the most important deity.

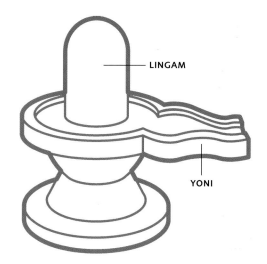

LINGAM

YONI

LINGAM

The term "lingam" derives from the Sanskrit word *linga*, meaning "mark" or "sign." It also means "phallus" and is the masculine symbol of procreation. The Shiva lingam is held in reverence in temples all over India. Shiva (see page 116) represents the primeval and invisible yet omnipresent energy of the creator. The Shiva lingam is a visible symbol of that energy, or ultimate reality, present in humans and in all creation. It is usually mounted on a circular or square receptacle called the *avudaiyar*, a symbol of the yoni or female principle.

YONI

The term "yoni" derives from the Sanskrit word meaning "place of birth" or "womb" and refers to the female sexual organ or vulva. In Hinduism, the yoni is a symbol of the goddess Shakti, the representation of feminine generative power. The yoni is often associated in the iconography of Shiva with the phallic lingam, Shiva's symbol. The lingam is depicted as resting in the *avudaiyar*, the spouted dish that represents the yoni. The two symbols together signify the eternal process of creation and regeneration.

TRISULA

The *trisula*, which means "three spear" in Sanskrit, is the three-pronged ceremonial weapon belonging to the Hindu deity Shiva (see page 116). Some mythic accounts say Shiva's *trisula* was used to sever the original head of the elephant god Ganesha, Shiva's son (see page 121). The goddesses Shakti and Durga also hold the *trisula* as a sacred weapon and as a symbol of their consort Shiva. The three points have various meanings and significance in Hindu mythology, representing the trifold aspects of the divine as creator, preserver, and destroyer; past, present, and future; and will, action, and wisdom. They can also symbolize the three *gunas* or tendencies: *sattva* (goodness), *rajas* (passion), and *tamas* (darkness). The *trisula* is reflected in the Buddhist symbol of the *triratna* (see page 132).

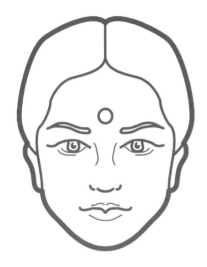

TILAK

The tilak, a mark applied to the forehead, is a visible sign that the person in question practices the Hindu religion. The tilak does not have a standard shape or color as it is applied differently by members of different Hindu sects and sub-sects. The mark is positioned between and slightly above the eyebrows, symbolizing the wearer's aspiration to cultivate higher consciousness in order to open up his or her mystical third eye. The most frequently worn type of tilak is the bindi, a decorative dot worn by women as a sign of marriage.

DIYA

Diya is a Sanskrit word meaning "lamp." A *diya* is a small clay lamp fuelled by oil, which is used in worship, particularly to celebrate Diwali, the Festival of Lights. *Diyas* are lit to pay homage to Lakshmi, the goddess of prosperity (see page 119), an important deity in the celebration of Diwali. Lighting a *diya* in each corner of the home is said to invoke the presence of the deity. Light—a symbol of hope—is said to banish evil and ignorance and bring prosperity to the home's inhabitants.

MANDALA

The term "mandala" derives from the Sanskrit for an enclosed space that is the abode of one or many deities. A mandala is usually drawn as a circular shape, but it can also be a square, a triangle, or a square within a circle. In the Hindu tradition, mandalas are used for meditation and the planning of buildings and sacred sites.

In spiritual practice, the mandala is drawn and/or mentally visualized by the meditator. The goal of the meditation is to merge with the deity represented by the space at the center of the mandala. As the meditator progresses from the outer rings toward the center, he or she imagines various stages of purification and realization. Ultimately, the meditator visualizes that his or her body is the mandala, which contains the entire universe. In this state of identification with the deity, the meditator understands that nirvana (the state of being free from both suffering and the cycle of rebirth) and samsara (the endless cycle of birth, death, and rebirth) are the same. Absorbed within the compassion and wisdom of the deity, the meditator can more easily transcend the limitations of the ordinary personality and achieve enlightenment. (See also page 127.)

SRI YANTRA

A yantra is another aid to meditation. It is made up of abstract geometric shapes and patterns and visually represents the harmonic tones of mantras, or sacred sounds, that are attributed to a particular deity. By focusing on the yantra while intoning mantras, the meditator invites the essence of these deities to penetrate his or her being.

The Sri Yantra, or Yantra of Creation, which is made up of nine interlinked triangles, is the most revered and perhaps the oldest of all the Hindu yantras. It symbolizes Shiva (see page 116) and Shakti, the male and female principles, as one totality. Shiva and Shakti join to produce the *bindu*, or the primordial seed of the universe, as represented by a point at the center of the yantra.

The Sri Yantra is believed to be the image of the Om mantra (see pages 125 and 363), thought to be the primordial sound of creation. Hans Jenny, the Swiss doctor and researcher (1904–1972), found that when Om is intoned into a tonoscope (a device he developed that transforms sound into a visual representation on a screen), it produces a Sri Yantra.

BRAHMA

Brahma the Creator, Vishnu the Preserver, and Shiva the Destroyer make up the Trimurti or Hindu trinity. Brahma the Creator has four heads, four faces, and four arms. With each head he continually recites one of the four Vedas. One of his hands holds a tool for making a sacrifice; another holds a water pot, symbolizing water as the source of life; in the third hand he holds a string of prayer beads that he uses to keep track of the universe's time; in the fourth he holds the Vedas, or holy scriptures.

SHIVA

Shiva the Destroyer or Transformer is one of the Hindu trinity and is often worshipped as the Shiva lingam (see page 111). He may be depicted in meditation, or represented as dancing upon the demon of ignorance in his manifestation as Nataraja, the Lord of the Dance. A god of masculinity, he is sometimes shown riding the bull Nandi (see page 123), a symbol of virility. He has a third eye and bears a crescent moon on his head. It is said that the Ganga River flows from his matted hair. His weapon is the *trisula*, or trident (see page 112).

VISHNU

In the Trimurti, the four-armed Vishnu is responsible for the preservation of the universe. He holds a lotus symbolizing reincarnation, a mace indicating strength, a conch shell (see page 265) to dispel demons, and a chakra (or energy center) for destroying evil. When the world is under threat, he can appear as the tortoise Kurma (see page 271) or the fish Matsya. His skin is blue, indicating his all-pervasive nature. The name Vishnu translates as "All-Pervading One" and indicates that he is not limited by space, time, or matter.

KRISHNA

Krishna, an incarnation of Vishnu, is easily recognizable by his image. His skin is dark blue and he wears a yellow silk dhoti or loincloth, with a feathered turban. A popular depiction shows him as a young man in a relaxed pose, one leg bent in front of the other, playing the flute. Known as the divine herdsman, he is often accompanied by cows. In his youth Krishna played the flute to seduce the daughters of cowherds and became known as a great lover. He represents the joyful and sometimes playful relationship between gods and humans.

KALI

Also called the Dark Mother, Kali is the Hindu Triple Goddess (see page 103) of creation, preservation, and destruction, now most known for her destroyer aspect. As Triple Goddess, everything in her world is created and destroyed in endless cycles. The mystical experience of Kali described by modern-day devotees is a glimpse into the formless state beyond death, where one returns to the Great Mother's womb to merge with her vast, oceanic being. Kali carries a severed head and wears a girdle of human arms and a necklace of skulls representing the destruction of ignorance.

PARVATI

Parvati, a representation of Shakti, or divine feminine power, is the female counterpart of and consort of Shiva (see page 116) and mother of Ganesha (see page 121). She symbolizes Hindu virtues such as fertility, marital felicity, devotion to a spouse, and power. The *Saundaryalahari*, a literary work that praises the grace and generosity of Parvati, states that only when Shiva is united with Shakti does he have the power to create. In Hinduism there is a perennial tension between the asceticism of Shiva and the secular householder ideal represented by Parvati.

LAKSHMI

The goddess Lakshmi, who is the female counterpart of the god Vishnu (see page 117), is the goddess of prosperity, purity, and generosity. Because Lakshmi represents good luck, women pray to her for the well-being and prosperity of their family. She has a golden complexion, four arms, and is seated on a lotus. Every year in autumn, on the brightest full-moon night, Bengalis believe that Lakshmi descends to earth on her mount, a great white owl, and removes poverty, stagnation, and laziness from their lives.

VARUNA

Varuna is a god of the sky, rain, and the celestial ocean, as well as the god of law and the underworld. He is the enforcer of contracts and punishes mortals who break their word by capturing them with his snakeskin noose. Varuna is light-skinned and is often depicted riding a *makara* or sea monster and wearing golden armor. In the *Rig Veda* Varuna was chief of the gods but in later times was overshadowed by Indra and became the god of oceans and rivers.

INDRA

Known as the god of war and weather and as King of the Gods, Indra is the chief deity in the sacred Hindu text, the *Rig Veda*. Indra's religious popularity diminished with the rise of the Trimurti (Brahma, Shiva, Vishnu, see page 116), but he remains significant in Indian mythology. He is a solar god, depicted with a golden body, jaw, and nails. Indra's weapons are the thunderbolt, the bow, and the lance, and he rides a four-tusked white elephant called Airavata. He is known for his heroic, impetuous, and amorous character.

YAMA

Yama, known as the Lord of Death, is an ancient god of Vedic mythology. He was said to have been the first human who died and found his way to the celestial abodes. Because of that achievement, he became god of the dead. In imagery he is depicted with green or red skin, red clothes, and riding a water buffalo. He holds a looped rope in his left hand, which he uses to pull the soul from the corpse. He is the son of the solar god Surya and the twin brother of the goddess Yami.

GANESHA

The elephant-headed deity, Ganesha, has the body of a human being, broken tusks, a huge trunk, and a vast belly. He is often seen riding a mouse or sitting on a lotus. Popularly held to be the son of Shiva (see page 116) and Parvati (see page 119), he is one of the best-known and most-loved gods in India. He is widely revered as the remover of obstacles and/or as the placer of obstacles for those who need to be thwarted. Known as Lord of Beginnings, he is invoked at the start of business ventures. He grants success, prosperity, and protection against adversity.

HANUMAN

Hanuman has the body of a man and the face and tail of a monkey. Along with Ganesha (see page 121) and Garuda (see page 124), he is one of the three Hindu gods with animalistic physical features. He is loved all over India as the monkey god who faithfully served Rama, an avatar of Vishnu (see page 117), in his war against the demon king Ravana. Hanuman is widely worshipped in northern India as a protector against evil and is revered for his immense strength and agility. He symbolizes pure devotion, complete surrender, and the absence of ego.

NANDI

The bull Nandi is the mount of the god Shiva (see page 116), as well as Shiva himself in his early animal form. In ancient times, Shiva was worshipped as a horned fertility deity. Today, the bull Nandi is considered Shiva's greatest devotee. Large statues of Nandi—depicted as a white, humped, and reclining bull—can be seen at the gate of most Shiva temples in India. His white color symbolizes purity, righteousness, and justice. When entering a Shiva temple, devotees always seek the blessings of Nandi before proceeding to worship Shiva. In everyday Indian speech the word *nandi* is used as a metaphor for a person blocking the way.

Because bulls symbolize sexual energy and fertility, Shiva riding on Nandi's back signifies the god's asceticism and his ability to master his bestial impulses. Nandi, whose name means "He who grants joy," also represents the inner strength that can be acquired through controlling one's violent and aggressive tendencies. Only those who have mastered their negative impulses and sexual desires, and achieved self-knowledge, can ride the bull like Shiva. (See also page 232.)

GARUDA

In Hindu mythology Garuda, a minor god in his own right, is the mount of the god Vishnu the Preserver (see page 117). Garuda has the body of a bird of prey, a human head with three eyes, an eagle's beak, and a crown. He is said to be large enough to block out the sun and symbolizes violent force, speed, and military power. Powerful warriors advancing against a weakened enemy are compared to Garuda swooping down on a serpent. He symbolizes the endless fight between good and evil.

SWASTIKA

Derived from the Sanskrit word *svastika*, meaning "lucky" or "auspicious object," the swastika symbolizes well-being. Because it faces all four directions, it represents the creator god Brahma (see page 116). The swastika is considered extremely holy and auspicious by all Hindus and is widely used as a decorative motif, seen throughout India on the sides of temples, on the doorways of houses, on gift items, on business letterheads, and on food packaging. The Hindu god Ganesha (see page 121) is often shown sitting on a bed of swastikas.

OM

Om, a Hindu sacred sound that is considered the greatest of all mantras, is spoken as an exclamation at the beginning and end of Hindu prayers, meditations, and religious rituals. From the 6th century CE, the written symbol Om marked the start of sacred texts or inscriptions. It is so important that the entire scripture known as the Mandukya Upanishad is devoted to its explanation. In the Tibetan script (see page 363), the Om syllable has a slightly different appearance to its Sanskrit form.

The Om syllable is composed of the three sounds A-U-M. The letter A represents creation that issues forth from the seed of the god Brahma; the letter U refers to Vishnu, who preserves the world by holding Brahma on a lotus above himself; and the letter M symbolizes Shiva, who breathes in so that all things disintegrate and are reduced, once again, to their essence (see pages 116–117).

Om is said to be the primordial sound present at the creation of the universe, which contains all other sounds, words, languages, and mantras. Om is held to be the root of the universe and its sound continues to hold everything together.

BUDDHISM

In Tibetan Buddhism, symbolism is central to meditation and prayer. Deities that are manifestations of various aspects of the Buddha, or enlightened mind, have rich symbolism attached to them. Visualization of these deities and their symbols is an important aspect of Tibetan Buddhist meditation practice. Using symbols, in which meaning and information are compressed into a non-verbal message, helps bypass the linear mind and hastens liberation. All forms of Buddhism teach ideas such as impermanence, emptiness (no-self), and karma.

STUPA

In pre-Buddhist India, stupas were hemispherical structures or monuments that contained the remains of temporal rulers. The Buddha noticed that these structures were built for kings and told his followers that they should also be built for awakened ones—those who had, through their own efforts, been released from samsara, the endless cycle of birth, death, and rebirth. But rather than simply house their remains, stupas were to be memorials that would inspire later generations to follow the example of the enlightened ones—and so the Buddhist stupa came to be a symbol of illumination or enlightenment.

Buddhist stupas evolved into large hemispherical mounds that may feature gateways, fenced-off enclosures, a square platform with railings on top of the mound,

and above that a parasol, canopy, or spire. There is often a circumambulatory path around the stupa. The 14 rings around the spire seen in later Tibetan stupas symbolize the 14 stages of the path to buddhahood. The oldest-known stupa still in existence is the Dhamek Stupa at Sanchi in India.

SAND MANDALA

The Tibetan Buddhist sand mandala (see also page 114), underscores the concept of impermanence—that all things in life are transitory. For when, after great effort, the highly intricate sand mandala is finished, and the accompanying rituals and meditations are complete, it is systematically destroyed.

In Old Tibet, sand mandalas were created from crushed semi-precious stones. In modern times, plain white stones are ground down to sand and dyed. A team of monks begins by drawing the outline of the complex round mandala. The Kalachakra Mandala, for example, represents 722 deities and also contains sophisticated geometric forms and motifs. After drawing the outline, the monks apply the sand granules using small funnels and scrapers, continuing until the drawing of the mandala is completely filled in—a process that usually takes several weeks.

The destruction of a sand mandala is a meditative ritual. The deity syllables, along with the other elements of the mandala, are removed in a specific order, until it has been completely dismantled. The sand is swept into a jar, which is then wrapped in silk and carried to a river, where the sand is released back into nature.

TRIKONA

The *trikona* is an equilateral triangle, a sign associated with the Buddha's mind. In paintings and carvings it is found as a mark on Buddha Vairocana's breast. A triangle of flame points downward to indicate power over all temptations. It is also a sign of omniscience and of the Adi-Buddha, the primordial Buddha who was present before anything else existed. When pointing upward and seated on its base, the *trikona* represents the yoni or female principle (see page 111), from which the world is manifest. Two *trikonas* forming a star indicate creative activity.

WREATH OF FLAMES

The space within a Buddhist mandala is considered to be free from earthly defilement and completely pure. The outside border of a mandala is visualized as a wreath of flames in the colors of the rainbow: red, yellow, white, green, and blue. All coarse matter and impure thoughts are incinerated in the wreath of flames, as the adept visualizes entering the mandala. The wreath of flames also functions to deny entry to the uninitiated. For Buddhists, fire and flames symbolize the wisdom that burns away ignorance.

WHEEL OF LIFE

The Wheel of Life—also known as *bhavachakra* or the Wheel of Becoming— is a symbolic blueprint of the functions of samsara, the continuous cycle of birth, death, and rebirth from which Buddhists seek liberation through enlightenment. Yama, Lord of Death (see page 121), holds the wheel with his hands, jaws, and feet. He signifies that death is certain and that attachment to anything in this life is futile.

The outer rim of the wheel is made up of the Twelve Interdependent Causes and Effects, which are: ignorance, conditioning, consciousness, name and form, the six sensory organs (eye, ear, nose, tongue, body, mind), touch, sensation, desire, grasping, becoming, birth, and decay and death. The six larger sections of the wheel represent the Six Realms of Existence, those of the gods, demigods, humans, animals, hungry ghosts, and hell beings. At the wheel's hub are the Three Poisons or Three Root Delusions, usually depicted as a pig (greed), a snake (hatred), and a rooster (ignorance).

In the upper corner of the wheel is an image of the Buddha pointing to a cloud, symbolizing that the way out of samsara is through enlightenment.

EYES OF THE BUDDHA

Often depicted on stupas (see page 126), the dramatic eyes of the Buddha, looking out in four directions, represent the all-seeing wisdom of the Buddha. The eyes may be accompanied by a circular mark on the forehead, the *urna*, which is often mistaken for the third eye. It appears as a concave circular dot, but actually represents a whorl of white hair which is the 31st of the 32 physical characteristics or marks of the Buddha. It symbolizes the emptiness and purity of all phenomena. The mark was said to project light rays to the deities in the god realms announcing that the Buddha was going to deliver teachings on earth. It also represented his power to illuminate the world. Out of compassion, the Buddha directed his light of wisdom to first pacify the suffering of beings in the lower realms.

Beneath the eyes, there is sometimes depicted what appears to be a nose or a question mark. This is actually the number one in Nepalese script. It symbolizes the non-dual nature of phenomenal appearance and the transcendent unity of all things.

FOOTPRINTS OF THE BUDDHA

Placing one's head at or under the feet of a guru was a ritual gesture of recognition and devotion that was commonplace in ancient India. The footprints of the Buddha, known as *buddhapada*, were one of the first representations of the Buddha in Buddhist art. The *buddhapada* are highly revered in all Buddhist countries and researchers have located more than 3,000 examples throughout Asia. These ancient artworks carved in stone are usually protected within a temple structure.

The Buddha's footprints generally depict a *dharmachakra* or Wheel of Dharma in the center, symbolizing the Buddha's teachings. They can also include other Buddhist symbols, such as the lotus (see page 134), the swastika (see page 124), and the *triratna*, the mark of the Three Jewels (see page 132). Some large *buddhapada* include all 32, 108, or 132 auspicious marks or characteristics of the Buddha.

According to Buddhist legend, after the Buddha attained enlightenment, his feet made an imprint in the stone where he stepped. Another legend states that after his birth, the infant Buddha took seven steps to announce his spiritual dominance of the universe.

THE THREE JEWELS

The Three Jewels of Buddhism (also called the Three Refuges or the Triple Gem) are Buddha, Dharma, and Sangha. One becomes a Buddhist by taking refuge in the Three Jewels.

Buddha—meaning Enlightened or Awakened One—refers to both the historical Buddha and to one's future Buddha, one's highest potential, the Buddha nature within one that is waiting to be developed. Dharma also has a twofold meaning and refers both to the teachings of the Buddha and to one's own development or progress on the path. Sangha represents the community of practitioners who have taken refuge in the Three Jewels of Buddhism and who are actively using the teachings to benefit themselves and others.

The Three Jewels are represented by the *triratna*, a simple three-branched shape that is similar in shape to the letter W. The *triratna* appears in early Buddhist art in various contexts, especially as one of the symbols on the *buddhapada* or footprints of the Buddha (see page 131). More elaborate *triratnas* include a *dharmachakra*, or Wheel of Dharma, symbolizing the Buddha's teachings, or a lotus flower, symbolizing enlightenment.

BODHI TREE

After wandering around India for six years in search of enlightenment, the Buddha rested in a forest not far from the city of Bodhgaya. It was then, while meditating under the Bodhi Tree, that he finally realized his true nature. It is believed that a descendant of the original tree still grows at Bodhgaya. Bodhi trees (also known as bo trees) are considered sacred by Hindus and Buddhists and are a well-known symbol for happiness, longevity, and good luck, as well as a reminder of the ultimate potential for enlightenment that lies within everyone. (See also page 284.)

DEER

Deer symbolize the Buddha's first teaching at Deer Park, a shady forest teeming with deer at Sarnath in India. In the Tibetan tradition, any monastery that holds the Kangyur and Tengyur collections of texts (originals and commentaries) would announce that fact by displaying deer on either side of its Wheel of Dharma on the monastery roof. Legend has it that, in a former incarnation, the Buddha offered his life in exchange for a pregnant doe that had been ordered to be slaughtered by the king. Deeply moved, the king gave Deer Park over to the entire herd.

THE EIGHT AUSPICIOUS SYMBOLS

RIGHT-SPIRAL CONCH SHELL

The right-turning spirals of the conch echo the celestial motion of the planets and stars. The curls on the Buddha's head spiral to the right, as does the *urna* (long curl) between his eyebrows (see page 130). In ancient India the conch was associated with the triumph of a hero. When blown, the conch represents the melodious, sweet, resonant voice of the spiritual hero Buddha. In Tibetan Buddhist monasteries, the conch is sounded to call monks to prayer rituals. (See also pages 140 and 265.)

LOTUS

The lotus represents the enlightened mind that grows out of the muddy waters of samsara. In Buddhism, the heart is said to be an unopened flower, but when a person develops the virtues of the Buddha, the lotus opens. The Buddha is often depicted sitting on lotus blossom. The white lotus symbolizes mental purity and is associated with White Tara. The red lotus represents love and compassion and is the flower of Avalokiteshvara. The blue lotus signifies wisdom and is associated with Manjushri. The pink lotus symbolizes the Buddha himself. (See also page 307.)

EIGHT-SPOKED WHEEL

The wheel is a symbol of the Buddha's teachings. It is also called the Wheel of Transformation, as a metaphor for the rapid personal change possible through exposure to the Dharma (see page 132). The eight spokes refer to the Eightfold Path of the Buddha: right view and right intention, which concern the acquiring of wisdom; right speech, right action, and right livelihood, which promote ethical conduct; and right effort, right mindfulness, and right concentration, which support mental development.

UMBRELLA

The umbrella protects from both rain and heat. In ancient India it was also associated with royalty. As a symbol, the umbrella protects from the damaging heat of negative emotions, desire, and other spiritually harmful influences. As a sign of royalty, the umbrella is depicted held aloft over the head of the Buddha, representing the bestowal of honor and respect. The Buddha, who is sheltered by the umbrella, is considered the center of the universe as well as its spiritual guide.

ENDLESS KNOT

The intertwined lines symbolize that all phenomena are interdependent and joined together in a closed cycle of karmic cause and effect. The endless knot also represents the infinite wisdom of the Buddha—without beginning and without end—and the union of compassion and wisdom. And it signifies the illusory character of time, because it is endless.

GOLDEN FISH

These fish symbolize happiness, freedom, fertility, and abundance. They also signify how the Dharma (see page 132) creates a state of fearlessness and protection while one swims in the everyday samsara, the ocean of suffering. The fish are described as migrating freely through the water, as they receive and give Buddhist teachings. The golden fish originated in pre-Buddhist times as a symbol of the two main sacred rivers of India, the Yamuna and the Ganges, which represent the lunar and solar channels in the body.

VICTORY BANNER

Early Buddhists adopted the Hindu victory banner as an emblem of the Buddha's enlightenment, heralding the triumph of knowledge over ignorance. It specifically denotes the Buddha's triumph over the demon Mara, personifying temptations on the path to enlightenment. Only after conquering obstacles such as passion, fear of death, pride, and lust could the Buddha proclaim victory over ignorance and achieve nirvana. Cylindrical victory banners of beaten copper are placed at the corners of monastery and temple roofs.

TREASURE VASE

The treasure or wealth vase is a round vessel with a short neck and a large jewel on top indicating that it holds treasure. It is a vase of inexhaustible wealth—however much is removed from it, it remains perpetually full. It symbolizes the spiritual abundance of the Buddha, a treasure that did not diminish, however much of it he gave away. In Buddhist cultures, sealed treasure vases, filled with precious and sacred substances, are used as offerings in rituals, or are buried on a mountain pass, or at the site of a spring, where they are thought to attract wealth and bring harmony to the environment.

THE EIGHT AUSPICIOUS SUBSTANCES

MIRROR

The purpose of the mirror is to enable one to see oneself clearly. In Buddhism, the mirror is a symbol of emptiness, as it reveals all that is reflected by it as void in essence. All objects in the world are shown to be without substance, as they really are. The mirror represents the Dharmakaya, or Truth Body, of the Buddha and corresponds to right intention, the second factor of the Eightfold Path (see page 135). It symbolizes wisdom.

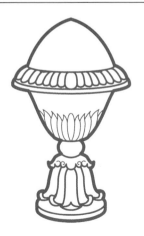

PRECIOUS MEDICINE

This is derived from the gallstones of cattle or elephants. Medically the gallstones, or bezoars, are said to be an antidote to poison and to alleviate fevers and contagious diseases. When mixed with honey and applied to the eyes, the bezoar bestows clear vision, in the spiritual sense. Precious medicine represents right mindfulness, the seventh factor of the Eightfold Path, which is an antidote to ignorance and the suffering it causes.

YOGURT

In ancient India, yogurt, or curd, was considered extremely nourishing and was an important part of the diet. Medically it functioned as a digestive and as a remedy for diarrhea. Its pure-white color symbolizes purity, spiritual nourishment, and the abandonment of negative actions and emotions. Before achieving enlightenment, the Buddha ended an austere fast with curd provided by Sujata, a farmer's daughter, which gave him the strength to meditate and achieve enlightenment. Yogurt corresponds to right livelihood, the fifth factor on the Eightfold Path.

DURVA GRASS

This grass is strong and hardy, with a knotty stalk—it was strong enough to use to bind bricks in ancient India. Durva grass was also combined with kusha grass to create meditation mats for religious ceremonies. It is thought that the Buddha sat on a mat made of durva and kusha grasses when he attained enlightenment under the Bodhi Tree (see page 133). Because it is known for its strength and durability, durva grass corresponds to right effort, the sixth factor on the Eightfold Path.

BAEL FRUIT

Bael fruit, or *bilva*, is also called wood apple because of its size and hard reddish-brown skin. In ancient India the bael was the most sacred of all fruit and the main offering in temples. It was highly regarded for its medicinal qualities, as a blood purifier, and a cure for dysentery. As a symbol, three bael are combined together, representing the Three Jewels (see page 132). The bael fruit symbolizes right action, the fourth element of the Eightfold Path (see page 135), which is known to bear good fruit in a spiritual sense.

CONCH SHELL

The right-spiral conch shell is also one of Buddhism's Eight Auspicious Symbols (see page 134) and represents the power of the Buddha's teachings. It is said that the great god Indra presented a conch shell to the Buddha in recognition of the superiority of his spiritual development and his teachings. It signifies right speech, the third factor on the Eightfold Path to enlightenment. (See also page 265.)

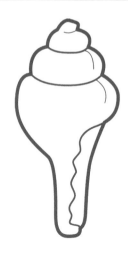

VERMILION POWDER

In India, vermilion (sometimes called cinnabar) is a red powder signifying power, love, or desire. It is known in Sanskrit as *sindura*, or sacred ash. It was used in Buddhist rituals and in the creation of sand mandalas (see page 127), as well as for the decoration of temples and monasteries. In Hindu culture, it is often used to create the tilak on the forehead (see page 113). In Buddhist symbolism, vermilion powder or *sindura* symbolizes right concentration, the eighth factor on the Buddha's Eightfold Path.

MUSTARD SEED

The Buddha instructed a woman who came to him distraught at the death of her child to bring him a white mustard seed from every home that had not experienced a death. Although mustard seed was common in every household, she returned empty-handed. In this way the Buddha showed her that she was not alone in experiencing death and that it is an inescapable part of life. The mustard seed therefore symbolizes right view, the first element of the Eightfold Path.

MUDRAS (HAND GESTURES)

DHARMACHAKRA MUDRA

Known as the teaching *mudra* or ritual hand gesture, the Dharmachakra Mudra originates from the Buddha's first teaching at Deer Park (see page 133) on the Four Noble Truths. The thumb and index finger form circles representing the Wheel of Dharma (see page 132). The hands are held in front of the heart, with right palm outward to represent the transmission of the teachings, and left palm facing inward to represent wisdom or internal realization. Many paintings of the Buddha and of the Buddhist masters display this *mudra*.

VARADA MUDRA

This is the boon-granting *mudra* of generosity. The hand is held open and downward with the fingers extended, and often rests on the knee of a seated Buddha or deity. The *mudra* symbolizes the bestowal of the realization of the two kinds of truths that coexist—conventional, common-sense, relative truth, and ultimate, absolute, or spiritual truth. It is found most often with deities that offer wish-granting jewels, fruits, or plants, such as the Medicine Buddha or White or Green Tara.

ABHAYA MUDRA

In the Abhaya Mudra, also known as a gesture of fearlessness, the right hand is slightly elevated and the palm turned outward. This *mudra* is used for protection, dispelling fear, bestowing blessings, and giving reassurance. It is sometimes called the gesture of renunciation, because it is associated with giving refuge and the process of formally becoming a Buddhist. The five extended fingers also represent the Five Perfections: generosity, morality, patience, effort, and meditative concentration.

BHUTADAMARA MUDRA

This *mudra*, a gesture of warding off evil, is also called the spirit subduer and awe-inspiring *mudra*. The hands are crossed at the wrist, right hand over the left, with the palms held outward, and the little fingers crossed, creating the image of wings. The middle fingers are held slightly bent. This *mudra* is used for protection and for the dispelling of demons.

VITARKA MUDRA

This is the gesture of communication, discussion or debate, and of the turning of the Wheel of Dharma (see page 132). The thumb and index finger of the right hand, held at shoulder level, touch forming a circle and the other fingers are extended upward. This is the mudra of the bodhisattva, one who aspires to become a Buddha in order to help other sentient beings and who helps them through reasoning, intellectual argument, and explanation of the teachings, as well as through great acts of compassion.

DHYANA MUDRA

This is the *mudra* of meditation and is said to be the one used by the Buddha when he achieved enlightenment under the Bodhi Tree (see page 133). This *mudra* represents concentration, balance, and tranquillity. The hands are held at stomach level or resting on the thighs, with the right hand placed above the left, palms facing upward, and fingers extended. The thumbs are held so that they touch at the tips and form a triangle that represents the Three Jewels of the Buddha, the Dharma, and the Sangha (see page 132).

BHUMISPARSHA MUDRA

This gesture is also called touching the earth, or the earth witness *mudra*. The right hand hangs down over the right knee, palm turned inward, with all five fingers extended and touching the ground. This mudra symbolizes the Buddha's victory over Mara when he achieved enlightenment under the Bodhi Tree (see page 133). With this *mudra* he summoned the earth goddess, Sthavara, to bear witness to his accomplishment.

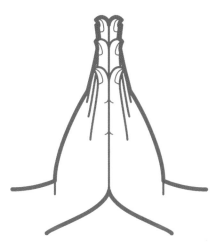

NAMASKARA MUDRA

Perhaps the oldest Indian hand gesture, the Namaskara Mudra represents a gesture of respectful greeting that acknowledges the divinity within the person being greeted. Its use is as common in India as the handshake is in Western countries. The gesture of palms folded together at the heart is a symbol of supplication, respect, and devotion to the Buddha and Buddhist deities. It can also indicate prayer and adoration. Followers and disciples of the Buddha are depicted practicing this mudra out of respect for the Buddha or a Buddhist master, but the gesture is not used by the Buddha himself.

TAOISM

Taoism may have roots in shamanism from as early as 2800 BCE, but really began in the 3rd or 4th century BCE with Lao Tzu, reputed author of the *Tao Te Ching*. Taoism teaches that the universe is governed by the Tao, or the Way, which is the dynamic interaction of yin (female principle) and yang (masculine principle). The Taoists also adopted the I Ching, or *Book of Changes*, which outlines a system of eight trigrams and 64 hexagrams (six-tier combinations) that symbolize the Taoist belief that the universe is in constant flux.

YIN AND YANG

The meaning of yin and yang is inherent in the famous black-and-white tai chi symbol. The circle around the outside represents the *wu chi*, or pregnant void, from which everything emerges—also known as the Tao, the Single Principle, the Great Void, and the One Supreme Unity. The Tao is

then divided into two opposite energy principles that interact with each other: yin (the black half) and yang (the white half).

The yang principle is considered more light, male (although a woman can also be yang or express yang qualities), expansive, upward-moving, active, and solar. The yin principle is thought to be more dark, female (although a man can also express be yin or express yin qualities), submissive, downward-moving, passive, and lunar. Within each half a small circle represents its opposite aspect, which reminds one that extreme yang will eventually become yin, and vice versa. The curving line represents the continuous interaction and movement between the dark and light, the negative and positive, and the male and the female. All is change; nothing is ever static or remains the same.

P'AN-KU

In Chinese mythology, P'an-ku was the first living being and the creator of the universe. In the beginning there was formless chaos. This chaos began to form into a cosmic egg. P'an-ku, a primitive, hairy giant, was born from the egg and set about creating the world. He separated yin from yang, creating the earth (yin) and the sky (yang, see opposite). P'an-ku stood on the earth and pushed up the sky, a task that took 18,000 years. When he died, his body became the natural elements of the earth.

SHOU-LAO

Shou-lao is a Chinese god of longevity and is often found painted on ceramics or in statue form. He is sometimes depicted as an old man holding a peach, the symbol of female genitalia connected with Taoist sexual mysticism, and with sexual practices that prolong life. In other forms he is depicted holding a staff, a scroll, and a gourd containing the elixir of life in one hand and a tree branch of the Peach of Immortality in the other. He wears a draped robe with a rope and tassels around his waist.

I CHING TRIGRAMS

CHIEN

TUI

This represents heaven, the sun, the creative impulse or idea, and the yang or male principle (see page 146). It represents the hidden creative potential that can be brought to light in any situation. It is identified with the cosmic viewpoint and the ruler or the sage who governs using power of insight. It is linked to the life-giving force of the sun, which sheds its light on the dark earth. Chien reminds us that the external, everyday world relies on a higher reality or power. It symbolizes the father in the family and the northwest direction. The part of the body represented is the head. Its animal is the horse, denoting power, force, and endurance, and its element is big metal.

This trigram represents true joy, as the serenity that arises from spiritual realization and a detached attitude. Inner harmony is arrived at through inner independence and the abandonment of desire. Tui signifies openness, a willingness to be led, and acceptance of life as it is. It calls for the ego to be denied its perennial grasping and for a return to harmony with the cosmos. The symbols of Tui are a marsh or a placid lake. The family member is the third daughter and the body part represented is the mouth. Its animal is the sheep, its direction is the west, and its element is small metal.

 **LI**

 **CHEN**

The clinging attitude of Li refers to the need to cling to the power of truth and to the potential for good to emerge when evil seems to be overtaking a person or situation. It represents reliance on the truths learned from the sages and not letting doubt take over. Li tells us that changing negative patterns formed over time takes slow, patient effort. Situations in our life will improve only to the extent that we improve ourselves. This trigram symbolizes fire, radiance, the south, and the second daughter. The body part represented is the eye. Its animal is the pheasant and its element is fire.

The arousing attitude of Chen is about learning to deal with the shocks of life. A shock occurs when we are forced to deal with long-term changes in our life, even seemingly positive ones like coming into a lot of money. When a crisis occurs— a death, a divorce, or job loss—it can be a wake-up call for positive change. Chen reminds one that, when jolted by life, it is important to keep one's inner balance and accept the challenges resulting from the new circumstance. Chen incites movement by taking initiative. It represents thunder, shaking, and the east. The family member represented is the first son and the body part is the foot. The animal of Chen is the dragon and its element is big wood.

 **SUN**

 **KAN**

The gentle, penetrating attitude of Sun represents the way the wisdom of the sages enters our lives. This trigram represents the mild but insistent way the wind penetrates the gaps around a window and the roots of a tree penetrate the earth. In this way, the sages' influence penetrates our subconscious until one day we see consciously with clarity. With consistent progress on the path to enlightenment, spiritual mysteries can be realized. Sun represents the entrance of a place or situation. Its direction is the southeast. The family member is the first daughter and the body part is the thigh. Its animal is the rooster and its element is small wood.

The abysmal attitude of Kan is one that gives up on slow steady perseverance on the spiritual path. An attitude of impatience and ambition, driven by want and fear, can create dangerous situations. Kan states that it is better to be path-oriented—and to abandon the abysmal attitude—than to be goal-oriented. If an abysmal situation arises, it is better to keep still until the correct solution reveals itself. When we strive for a particular solution that we want to happen, we abandon the slow steady spiritual work that results in enduring positive change. The symbol of Kan is a gorge and its direction is the north. The family member is the second son and the body part is the ear. The animal of Kan is the pig and its element is water.

 **KEN**

 **KUN**

The keeping-still attitude of Ken symbolizes a mountain, stillness, and being bound. People who are childish think only in terms of what they want and need and what they don't like and want to avoid. They think endlessly about goals and whether these are being met. Ken encourages quieting frenetic mental activity and renouncing the childish heart. The keeping-still attitude symbolizes meditation and abiding in a relaxed and awake state. Ken symbolizes standing still and the completion stage of an activity or situation. Its direction is the northeast. The family member is the third son and the body part represented is the hand. Its animal is the dog and its element is small earth.

This trigram represents the feminine attitude. It symbolizes the receptive, absorbing, nurturing power of the earth, the mother, and the belly. It represents devotion and the ability to yield to the teaching of the sages or to one's higher self or a higher power. We are receptive when we allow ourselves to be guided by the moment. If we are receptive, we detach from wanting friends or family to be otherwise when they are unfaithful or insensitive, and we forgo vindictiveness or self-pity. We never give up on them and give them time to return to correct their behavior. The animal of Kun is the cow, denoting the feminine and receptive aspects of a personality or situation. Its direction is the southwest and its element is big earth.

THE EIGHT IMMORTALS

CHUNG-LI CHUAN

At 1,800 years old, Chung-li Chuan is said to be the oldest of the Eight Immortals. His symbol is a fan that is made of feathers or a palm leaf and has the ability to revive the dead. He frequently visits earth as a messenger of the gods mounted on a Chi Lin, a mythical animal sacred to Taoists. As a baby, he has distinctive features: a high-domed head, a massive brow, large ears, and arms as long as a three-year-old's. As an adult, he is usually depicted as bearded, overweight, with a bare chest, and holding a fan. His hair is gathered in two coils on the sides of his head. He is also called Master of the Cloud-Chamber. When brought into the home, his image is said to produce a family of honorable sons and to invoke the support of the Tai Sui (also known as the Grand Duke Jupiter or the Grand Commander of the current year). Chung-li Chuan's image will appease the Tai Sui if you have offended him and will save you from misfortune. His direction is east and his element is wood.

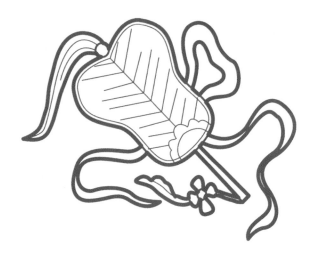

HO HSIEN-KU

At the age of 14, Ho Hsien-ku became immortal when she was given the precious Peach of Immortality. Soon afterward she was visited by a deity and vowed to remain a virgin. A magical lotus blossom is the symbol of her power and purity. Ho Hsien-ku is depicted as an attractive young woman dressed in beautiful robes or sometimes in the leafy cape and skirt worn by the Immortals. Instead of a lotus blossom she may carry a large ladle, with a bowl made of woven bamboo filled with fruits and plants associated with Taoist immortality, such as magic fungus, peaches, pine needles, and narcissus flowers. Alternatively, she may hold a basket of mountain fruits and herbs gathered for her mother. Ho Hsien-ku is depicted sitting on a deer, which is a symbol of high-strung energy and longevity. Taoists believe that Ho Hsien-Ku is still alive, but is now more than 1,400 years old. She helps those who are in desperate situations and in need of divine intervention. She is invoked for a happy marriage and brings a family good luck. Her direction is the southwest and her element is earth.

CHANG KUO

Chang Kuo is recognized by his musical instruments, a fish-drum or long castanets. He also carries a tube that contains phoenix feathers used for forecasting good fortune or impending misfortune. He is thought to help those who have passed on to have a better rebirth in one of the good realms. He rides a white donkey that is his beloved companion. He is so close to this donkey that when he is depicted without his mount, a miniature image of the donkey will appear somewhere next to him. Chang Kuo would ride his donkey, traveling great distances in a day. When he stopped to rest, he would magically fold up his donkey until it was no thicker than paper, and slip it into his cap. When he wanted to ride the donkey, he would rehydrate it by squirting water at it from his mouth. When Chang Kuo's image is placed in a bedroom, he helps those trying to have children and is said to give the gift of prophetic dreams. His direction is north and his element is water.

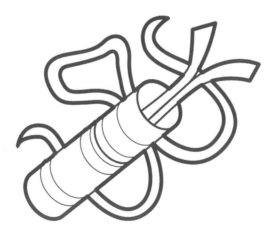

LU TUNG-PIN

The symbol of Lu Tung-pin is a double-edged demon-slaying yang sword, which was given to him by a dragon. He carries the sword on his back and it enables him to hide in the heavens and make himself invisible to evil spirits. Lu Tung-pin is represented as a dignified elderly man dressed as a scholar and he is the literary member of the group of Eight Immortals. His beard is divided into three parts, symbolizing his knowledge and use of the three mystical channels in the body for accessing the highest meditative states. As the patron saint of jugglers, magicians, and barbers, he is called the Ancestor Lu. Believed to have lived for 400 years on earth, he is one of the most popular of the Immortals and is portrayed more often than any of the others. Two large Taoist literary works are devoted to his life. When he is invoked in a home setting, he keeps from entering those who would have evil intentions. His direction is west and his element is metal.

HAN HSIANG-TZU

Han Hsiang-tzu is recognized by his magical flute, on which he plays the Six Healing Sounds, and by his long castanets. The flute is made of purple bamboo that glows in the dark. He wears the leafy cap and deerskin skirt of the Immortals and rides an ox. At times he is shown with a small furnace to indicate his skill as an alchemist. Han Hsiang-tzu was thought to be wild and irresponsible and was banished for strongly criticizing the king's veneration of a bone, a sacred relic of the Buddha. He was so skilled that he was able to fill empty wine goblets by speaking the "wizard word" and could cause flowers to spring up and bloom by his mere intention. He was recognized as an expert on the mysteries of heaven and a master of the Five Phases of Energy. His robe bore sacred knots that were symbols of his achievement of combining yin and yang energy (see page 146) into the original Primordial Energy. His direction is southeast and his element is wood.

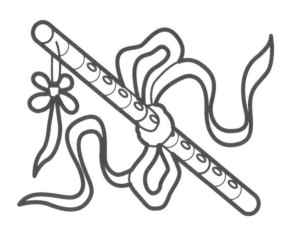

TSAO KUO-CHIU

Recognized by his magical castanets, Tsao Kuo-chiu plays them to facilitate meditation and transport himself through the universe. His mount is the Pi Yao, a magical animal that helps him penetrate the secrets of the Tao. The uncle of one of the Sung emperors, he was so deeply ashamed that his nephew, the emperor, put people to death that he retreated to the mountains, where he meditated and studied Taoist principles. He wore rustic clothing and a leafy cap, frequently going without food for ten days at a time. While there he met two Immortals who questioned him about what he was trying to accomplish. Impressed by his answers, they taught Tsao Kuo-chiu how to be in perfect harmony with nature and then invited him to join them. Having his image in the home is said to invoke his powerful protection. He provides excellent support for students who want to be successful in their studies. His direction is northeast and his element is earth.

LI TIEH-KUAI

Li Tieh-kuai is recognized by his iron crutch, his hideous, deformed body, and his magical gourd that exudes a vapour in which sometimes appears an image of his *hun*, or soul. Li Tieh-kuai told his pupil that his *hun* was going on a journey to see Lao Tzu, but that his *p'o*, or earthly material body/soul, would remain with the pupil. The pupil, tired of waiting, burned the body and Li Tieh-kuai returned to find it gone. Seeing the corpse of a starved beggar he entered into it, thus gaining his hideous body. Having mastered the Five Phases and yin and yang energies (see page 146), he is able to transform matter and produce medicine from his gourd. Li Tieh-kuai is known for his compassion and his generosity for those who are recovering from illness. He can transform himself into a dragon and fly into the heavens, but he will return to earth when invoked by those in need. When in human form, his mount is a Pi Yao, the mythical guardian animal known for its dignity and courage. His direction is south and his element is fire.

LAN TSAI-HO

Represented as a youth and old man, or as a girl, Lan Tsai-ho is the youngest of the Immortals (even in old age, his appearance remains youthful). His symbol is his magical flower basket, which is said to contain 108 plants, flowers, and tree branches associated with longevity. They include magical fungus, sprigs of bamboo, pine, and plum, and chrysanthemums. He is known for his ragged gown with black wooden buttons. One of his feet has a shoe, while the other foot is bare. His mount is an elephant, a symbol of wisdom, strength, and prudence, and he is also associated with the crane. It is said that one night, while Lan Tsai-ho was drinking in a tavern, he heard a flute. Entranced by the beautiful sound, he soared into the sky mounted upon a crane, and disappeared from sight. Having an image of him in the home is said to bring joyousness to family life and attract kind and beautiful people as guests. His direction is northwest and his element is metal.

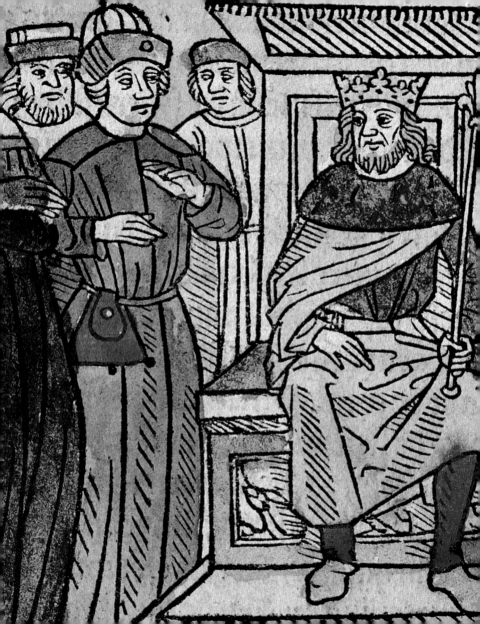

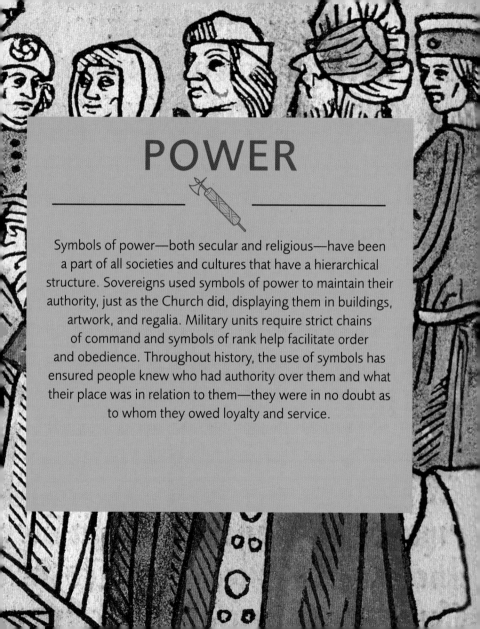

POWER

Symbols of power—both secular and religious—have been a part of all societies and cultures that have a hierarchical structure. Sovereigns used symbols of power to maintain their authority, just as the Church did, displaying them in buildings, artwork, and regalia. Military units require strict chains of command and symbols of rank help facilitate order and obedience. Throughout history, the use of symbols has ensured people knew who had authority over them and what their place was in relation to them—they were in no doubt as to whom they owed loyalty and service.

ROYALTY AND THE CHURCH

Symbols of power accompanied royalty and were displayed prominently in important royal buildings. Similarly, members of the Church hierarchy made use of symbols to indicate their power over ordinary worshippers. The coronation of a ruler or king involved symbols of his rule, such as the crown and scepter, which often gave him power in the religious sphere as well. In Christianity—whether Protestant or Catholic—religious symbols demarcated those who were ordained as priests and bishops from the laity. The symbols of the Church, such as the various religious robes and headgear, the ring on a cardinal's hand, or a bishop's crosier, are comforting and reassuring to a congregation that desires guidance by an ordained clergy.

CROWN

A crown is the traditional head covering worn by a monarch or a deity (such as Christ the King), which symbolizes elevation, power, and authority (both temporal and divine). Often having bejeweled points or spikes pointing upward, a crown sits on the "crown" of the head and connects the earthly person wearing it with the divinity of the heavens above. The circle of the crown symbolizes perfection or "crowning achievement." The crown passed from the monarch to his or her successor, symbolizing the continuity of the monarchy.

DIADEM

A diadem (from the Greek word *diadein*, "to fasten") was a white ribbon tied around the crown of the king's head, representing his power. It was knotted at the base of the neck and the ribbon's two long ends were draped on the king's shoulders, denoting his authority. Later the term was used to denote a wreath made of plant material or a circular crown made of metal. A diadem can also be a tiara, a jeweled ornament in the shape of a half-crown that is worn by women.

BELL

Bells summon the faithful to prayer and services. They were originally used to call worshippers to Mass in the Roman catacombs. From the 6th century CE onward, monastery texts mention the use of larger bells and by the end of the Middle Ages very large bells were being cast for use in churches. Bells reminded the faithful to turn toward God, but they also functioned to drive away evil spirits and keep the devil from taking a human soul. They also played a part in exorcisms and excommunication rites.

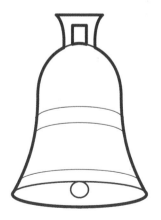

KEYS

Keys symbolize the administrative authority of the papacy of the Catholic Church. The keys were handed down from St. Peter, the first Pope, who was given the keys to the kingdom of heaven by Christ (see also page 77). They stand for the connection between heaven and earth, and the Church's power to "lock" the faithful into the teachings of Jesus Christ. They also symbolize the infallibility of the Pope on matters of faith or morals. The power of the keys is the power to bind and loose, the authority to absolve sins, and make doctrinal judgements.

RING

Bishops in many Christian denominations wear an ecclesiastical ring signifying their union with the Church and their fidelity to its teachings and traditions. The papal ring, or Fisherman's Ring, is bestowed on the Pope when he is anointed. Catholic nuns also wear a simple wedding ring, signifying their marriage or consecration to God and Christ. In the coronation ceremony for monarchs, the sovereign and his or her consort often receive a ring blessed by the highest prelate in the land.

CROSIER

Those holding high office in the Roman Catholic, Eastern Orthodox, and Anglican Churches carry a crosier, an ornate staff made of gold or silver, resembling a shepherd's crook. It is presented to the prelate at his consecration. When the bishop or cardinal walks in procession, confers sacraments, or gives blessings, he carries the crosier in his left hand. It signifies that the bearer is the shepherd, or spiritual guide, of his congregation. The pointed ferule at the base symbolizes his duty to prod his flock into a more spiritual

life. The crook represents his responsibility to pull back in those who have strayed from the path. The staff itself signifies his steadfast support of the members of his Church (see also page 237).

The Eastern Orthodox crosier is shaped like a crutch, with arms curving down and a very small cross on top. A rectangular piece of brocade or velvet, called a sudarium, embroidered with a religious symbol, hangs below the arms. Some Eastern crosiers are topped with a pair of serpents or dragons.

PAPAL CROSS

The papal cross, also called a ferula, is an emblem of papal office. It has three horizontal bars of diminishing length as they move toward the top. The crossbars have been said to represent the three crosses on Calvary or the Holy Trinity. Others say that the cross echoes the elaborate, three-tiered papal crown. It is probably derived from the Cross of Lorraine, which has two horizontals and was used by archbishops in medieval Christianity. The added third horizontal indicates the higher rank of the Pope.

MACE

The ceremonial mace, a highly ornamented, short staff usually made of metal, is a symbol of authority in both secular and religious settings. In civil ceremonies, a mace-bearer carries the mace ahead of the sovereign or high official. The use of the ceremonial mace can also be found in parliamentary, formal academic, and papal processions.

ORB

The sovereign's orb, or *globus cruciger*, is a small ball topped with a cross. The orb was used as a symbol of authority throughout the Middle Ages to symbolize Christ's dominion over the world. When the orb is depicted as being held by Christ himself, he is referred to as *Salvator Mundi*, or Savior of the World (see page 79). Monarchs are shown holding the orb in their left hand.

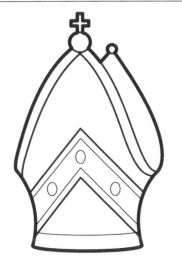

MITER

The miter is ceremonial, religious headgear worn by Christian bishops. This tall, folding cap consists of two segments, front and back, that rise to a peak and are sewn together at the sides. The use of the miter dates from Greco-Roman times, when it was worn by high priests as a symbol of spiritual power.

SCEPTER

A scepter is a symbolic ornamental staff held by a ruling monarch, usually in the right hand, representing royal authority. It was used in ancient Greece by respected elders as a symbol of their authority and later came to be used by a range of government officials, such as judges and military leaders. The British Crown Jewels include two scepters.

SWORD

In the Christian tradition, the sword is an emblem of the Archangel Michael. Cherubs with flaming swords were placed by God at the gates of paradise after the fall of Adam and Eve. When a British monarch is crowned, he or she is presented with the Sword of State and later with the Sword of Spiritual Justice, the Sword of Temporal Justice, and the Sword of Mercy.

SCALLOP SHELL

The scallop shell is the symbol of baptism in the Christian church and is often used to pour water over the baby's head. Representations of scallop shells often adorn baptismal fonts. The scallop shell is also the emblem of St. James the Greater and is popular with those who make the pilgrimage, called the Way of St. James, to his shrine at Santiago de Compostela in Spain. The Way of St. James has existed for over a thousand years and was one of the most important Christian pilgrimages during medieval times. Pilgrims wore scallop shells as ornaments to symbolize the completion of a pilgrimage. One legend associated with the Way of St. James suggests that the route was originally a pagan fertility pilgrimage and scallop shells were carried as a symbol of fertility.

THE MILITARY

Military symbols represent the power and authority of the forces that protect the inhabitants of a country. Highly disciplined military hierarchies are defined by strict codes of conduct, a ranking system, regimented ceremonial activities such as marches and parades, and an award system for extraordinary valor. Complex symbols of rank are worn on uniforms and usually consist of braids, pins, or other markings on collars and cuffs, and epaulettes on the shoulders. Awards for bravery in service appear as a variety of medals with ribbons attached. Their color and design have special significance, such as the Purple Heart awarded to military personnel in the United States and the blue and white ribbon of the Distinguished Service Cross awarded to Royal Navy officers in the United Kingdom. Other military symbols include banners, ceremonial maces, swords, and other weapons.

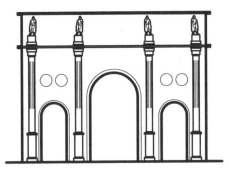

TRIUMPHAL ARCH

This free-standing monumental structure with two huge piers connected by an archway is built to celebrate a victory in war. First conceived and built by the Romans, triumphal arches were revived during the Renaissance. Later, Louis XIV (1638–1715) and Napoleon Bonaparte (1769–1821) built arches to commemorate military victories, the most famous being the Arc de Triomphe in Paris. Built to honor President Kim Il-Sung (1912–1994), the Arch of Triumph in Pyongyang is modeled on the Parisian Arc de Triomphe and is the largest arch in the world.

OAK-LEAF CLUSTERS

The oak tree, oak leaves, and the acorn, which are often found on military tombs, symbolize power, authority, and victory. An oak-leaf cluster is a symbol used on US military awards and decorations to denote those who have received an award more than once; the number of clusters indicates the number of subsequent awards of the decoration. In British Commonwealth countries, a bronze oak leaf signifies a Mention in Despatches. (See also page 283.)

ARROWS AND ARROWHEADS

Used as a military symbol, arrows and arrowheads represent military defense. Throughout history, the bow and arrow were formidable weapons and symbolized power and swift response to an attack. Native American Cheyenne warriors regarded their medicine arrows as symbols of their masculinity. And the Greek god Heracles battled the three-headed monster Geryon using his bow and arrow.

BATTLEAXE

Designed as a lethal weapon, the battleaxe is lighter than a utility axe, with a thinner blade. It was wielded in one or both hands. Since the late Neolithic era, axes have had a dual meaning, with both military and mystical significance. In the Celtic tradition, the axe symbolized a deity, chief, or warrior and it also represented authority and military duty. Native Americans, the Chinese, and the Celts called axes "thunder stones," recognizing that they were closely associated with both the power of destruction and the power of creation.

BANNER

In a military context, the banner, bearing the coat of arms of the owner, identified him and denoted his status or rank. It marked the rallying point for the battle and functioned as a symbol of victory. In some coats of arms, a banner is depicted in the design. Medieval English dragon banners, carried into war, were dragon windsocks attached to a carrying staff through the dragon's nostrils and front paws. The dragon banners would whistle eerily as the wind blew through them, spreading unease in the enemy ranks.

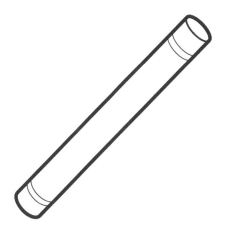

BATON

The baton is a symbol of authority dating back to Roman times when the short white baton was given to a military legate as a symbol of the imperial power entrusted to him. When he was invested with the baton, he held it above his head and said, "Above your head and mine"—meaning that he accepted his right to represent the authority of the emperor, which was the supreme authority in the land. In modern times the baton is also called a billy club or a nightstick and may be carried by law-enforcement officers.

SWORD

The sword has dual symbolism, as both an aggressive weapon and a defensive or protective one. Some swords were so finely crafted for the ideal weight, balance, and beauty that they were said to have magical powers. One famous example is Excalibur, the sword of King Arthur. The sword is a symbol of military honor and is used in England for the ceremonial knighting of those who have given outstanding service to queen and country. In Buddhism, the sword symbolizes the ability to cut through ignorance.

FASCES

A symbol of the Roman Republic, the fasces is a bundle of white birch rods tied together into a cylinder with an axe bound in among the rods, its blade projecting from the bundle. As rods bound together are harder to break, they symbolize strength through unity. They also represent the authority to punish citizens, while the axe stands for the authority to execute or protect them—whatever is needed. Italian Fascism derived its name from the fasces, but the symbol is widely used around the world, including on the cover of the French passport.

SHIELD

The shield is an ancient tool of the warrior, used for protection from missiles such as spears and arrows, and from blows delivered by a sword or mace. Once constructed of wood, metal, or animal hide, the shields used by modern-day police are made of synthetic materials. A shield symbolizes protection and its weight and form are determined by the kind of attacks it meets on the battlefield. Shields can be combined to create a protective wall, symbolizing that people can unite to defend themselves against a common enemy.

HAMMER AND SICKLE

The hammer is a symbol of the industrial worker, while the sickle is the symbol of the agricultural worker. Together they formed the emblem of the former Soviet Union and of international Communism. The hammer and sickle represented the hope of the ordinary worker to live a better and more humane life, but came to symbolize to many Westerners the excesses and extremes of the failed Communist regime.

LANCE

The lance, as well as the arrow (see page 171) and sword (see page 173), is a masculine symbol representing solar consciousness. Sometimes known as the blade, it is joined with the cup or chalice (see page 98) to represent the union of male and female. It is associated with chivalry, knights, and the Holy Grail (see page 80). Knights who were unattached and hired as mercenaries were known as "freelance." The lance is a symbol of victory and of the Hindu god of war, Indra (see page 120). It also signifies an experienced soldier or warrior. In the Christian tradition, St. George used a lance to slay the dragon.

HERALDRY

The practice of designing and recording coats of arms and badges originated in the Middle Ages. As the faces of knights in jousting contests were covered by steel armor, they began to wear badges and carry banners with their own unique colors and symbols. In early battles, messengers or heralds recorded the designs worn by the combatants so that they could announce the outcome. This heraldic record became the basis of the almost 900-year-old system of blazoning arms—coats of arms and their accessories being known as "blazon." The system, which recorded the symbols and colors that a family could use on a coat of arms, is still in use today.

MARKS OF CADENCY

By the late Middle Ages heraldry was a well-established practice across Europe, regulated by professional heralds. A family would include its coats of arms on banners, fireplace mantels, garments, and stained-glass windows to advertise the family pedigree. The arms of all family members had to be similar to those used by its oldest surviving member (the plain coat), but by the 15th century marks of cadency were being added to indicate the status of the sons.

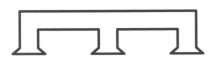

LABEL OF THREE POINTS—ELDEST SON, FIRSTBORN DURING THE LIFETIME OF THE FATHER

CRESCENT—SECOND SON

MULLET—THIRD SON

MARTLET—FOURTH SON

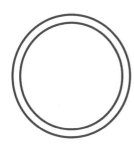

ANNULET—FIFTH SON

FLEUR-DE-LIS—SIXTH SON

ROSE—SEVENTH SON

CROSS MOLINE—EIGHTH SON

DOUBLE QUATREFOIL—NINTH SON

FURS AND SHIELDS

The heraldic system includes a description of the escutcheon (shield or lozenge), the crest, and (if present) supporters, family mottoes, mythical beasts, and other insignia. The design of the coat of arms is called the "charge" and might include "ordinaries" such as simple stripes and crosses or an animal such as a lion or dragon. The animals were depicted in standardized positions that had symbolic meaning. Patterns known as "furs" were also used and had their own significance. The rules of heraldry differ from country to country, but some aspects are consistent. Personal heraldry is legally protected and continues to be used around the world, and many cities and towns in Europe and elsewhere in the world also make use of arms.

ERMINE

Ermine, the most widely used fur in heraldry, is the pure-white winter coat of the stoat, which had a black tail. When the skins were sewn together, they would create a luxurious white fur garment with a pattern of small black marks, called ermine spots. The winter stoat symbolizes purity or virginity. Legend has it that the ermine was so protective of its pure-white coat that it would die rather than let it become soiled. This came to represent the noble Christian desire to choose to die rather than be blemished by sin.

VAIR

In heraldry, vair originated from the fur of a species of squirrel with a blue-gray back and a white belly. When sewn together, the colored furs were alternated, so the vair pattern consists of rows of small, equal-sized bell-like shapes of alternating blue and white. There are older variations, with the bells of each tincture lined up in columns rather than alternating. The word "vair" may originally have meant "varied," because it was commonly used to describe horses with a mottled pattern.

SHIELD AND LOZENGE

The correct term in heraldry for the shield in a coat of arms is "escutcheon" (not "crest"). The shield or escutcheon carried the design, or charge. The term "escutcheon" can also be used to refer to a family and its honor. The "black sheep" in the family might be described as a "blot on the escutcheon."

The shape of the escutcheon is based on the shields that knights used during the Middle Ages. Since the shield is a device used in battle, it was only appropriate for men. Women would bear their arms upon a diamond-shaped lozenge or on a rhombus standing on one of its acute corners. The exception was the queen, who used a male escutcheon. Clergymen bore their arms on an oval shield.

Only the king or queen could grant permission to carry a coat of arms, which initially were granted solely to knights and members of the nobility. Later, merchants and craftsmen were allowed to have a coat of arms, the charge depicting their trade.

TINCTURE

Tincture, or color, is an important aspect of heraldry. The tinctures all had special names, many of which were derived from the Norman French tradition. The metals used were gold and silver, while the six main colors were red, blue, black, purple, white, and green. Each metal and color had a symbolic meaning.

METALS

GOLD (OR)
Gold symbolizes generosity and elevation of mind.

SILVER/WHITE (ARGENT)
Silver symbolizes peace and sincerity.

COLORS

RED (GULES)
Red is the sign of a warrior or martyr, indicating courage, military strength, and generosity.

PURPLE (PURPURE)
Purple is a sign of sovereignty, royalty, and justice.

BLUE (AZURE)
Blue stands for truth and loyalty.

WHITE
White is a sign of honor.

BLACK (SABLE)
Black indicates constancy or grief.

GREEN (VERT)
Green stands for hope, joy, and loyalty.

HERALDIC ANIMAL STANCES

RAMPANT

This is one of the most common attitudes
for heraldic animals. The lion rears up on
its hind legs, standing on its left leg, with
its forelegs lifted ready to strike. The right
paw is usually above the left. The body
generally faces the sinister or left side.

PASSANT

The animal's body faces the sinister side,
with only the right foreleg raised, as if
stepping forward. The beast is striding
confidently, resolute, and determined.

STATANT GUARDANT

In this attitude the beast is in a standing position, with all paws on the ground, the tail erect, and the head facing toward the viewer. It symbolizes being alert and ready for battle.

SALIENT

The beast, in the sinister position, is leaping or springing forward toward its prey. Its hind feet are planted on the ground and the right foreleg is lifted slightly higher than the left. Symbolizing a willingness to charge the enemy in battle, the salient attitude symbolizes both fearlessness and valor.

ESOTERIC AND MAGICAL TRADITIONS

The word "magic" comes from the Greek *magikos*, referring to the Magians, the Zoroastrian astrologer-priests of ancient Mesopotamia. The practice of magic existed in ancient Egypt, Mesopotamia, and Persia, but was restricted to those who were initiated into its mysteries. Because magic was a form of power, over the centuries it remained a hidden practice whose secrets were guarded by various esoteric groups. If an initiate went through a demanding rite of passage, he or she would then be introduced to magical symbols and practices that were unknown to outsiders. Alchemy, astrology, and ceremonial magic all have their own esoteric symbols.

ALCHEMY

A precursor to modern-day chemistry, alchemy dates back at least 2,500 years. Its origins can be found in the esoteric practices of Greece and Rome, Persia, India, Mesopotamia, Egypt, China, Japan, and Islamic civilizations. This early multi-disciplinary practice combined chemistry, metallurgy, medicine, astrology, mysticism, and art. Viewed by outsiders as the practice of creating gold, alchemy was in reality focused on spiritual enlightenment. Carl Jung compared it to the process of individuation, in which a person explores the dark material of the unconscious mind, integrates it on a conscious level, and achieves psychological maturity and spiritual insight. Because the Church deemed alchemy heretical, alchemists used symbols to disguise their work.

PHILOSOPHER'S STONE

This representation of humankind's wholeness symbolizes the fierce desire to be one in mystical union with God, within one's own soul. In alchemy, the Philosopher's Stone is not a physical stone, but a legendary substance capable of turning base metal into gold. Ultimately, this was the most sought-after goal in alchemy. It was also believed to be an elixir of immortality and, once made or achieved, could never be lost. The Philosopher's Stone thus became a metaphor for the inner potential of a human being to evolve from a lower state of imperfection (symbolized by base metals) to a higher state of enlightenment and perfection (symbolized by gold). In this view, the transmutation of metals and the spiritual transmutation, purification, and rejuvenation of the body were one and the same. The Philosopher's Stone may be represented abstractly or by a pair of lions or a man and woman riding on lions.

HERMES TRISMEGISTUS

Hermes Trismegistus is the combined form of the Egyptian god Thoth and the Greek god Hermes, both gods of writing and magic in their respective cultures. During the Renaissance the Greek writings attributed to Hermes Trismegistus from the 2nd and 3rd centuries CE were compiled into the *Corpus Hermeticum* and became known as Hermetica. The original source of these writings, said to contain secret wisdom, may have been an Egyptian movement that represented a marginal sect within the Greco-Roman cultures. Most of the texts are presented as a dialogue (a popular teaching form in ancient times), in which Hermes-Thoth enlightens a confused disciple. The subject matter deals with alchemy, magic, and concepts reminiscent of Gnosticism (see page 92) and Neoplatonism.

The recovered Hermetic writings gave rise to mystical practices all over the world. Hermetic philosophy provided the individual with a way to transform one's base physical nature into higher realms. Today, the "Hermetic tradition" refers to alchemy, magic, astrology, and other occult subjects and practices.

MATERIALS USED IN THE ALCHEMICAL PROCESS

Alchemists make use of the innate qualities of the huge range of materials they employed in their experiments. Each substance is represented by an alchemical symbol. The following pages provide examples of some of these substances and symbols.

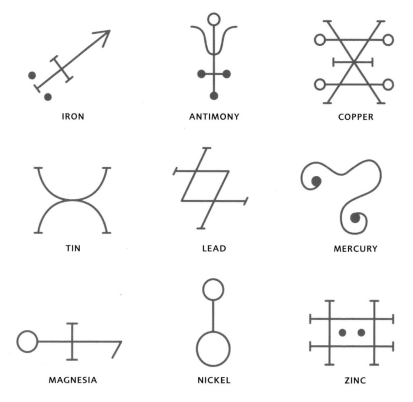

IRON

ANTIMONY

COPPER

TIN

LEAD

MERCURY

MAGNESIA

NICKEL

ZINC

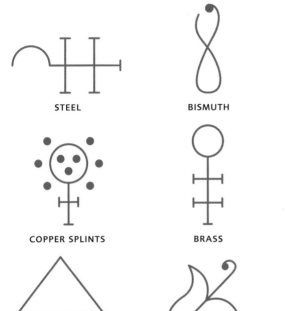

STEEL

BISMUTH

IRON FILINGS

COPPER SPLINTS

BRASS

GLASS

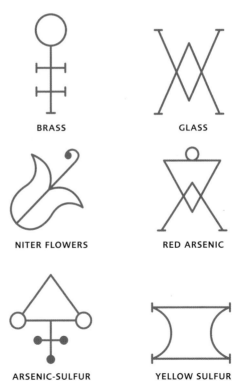

SULFUR

NITER FLOWERS

RED ARSENIC

WHITE ARSENIC

ARSENIC-SULFUR

YELLOW SULFUR

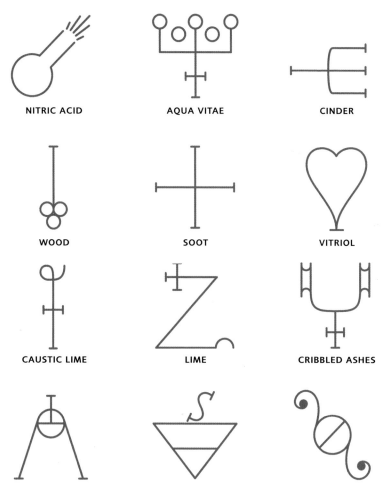

NITRIC ACID

AQUA VITAE

CINDER

WOOD

SOOT

VITRIOL

CAUSTIC LIME

LIME

CRIBBLED ASHES

CRYSTAL

CLAY

BORAX

ALUM

SOAPSTONE

BURNED PEBBLES

GRAVEL

BURNED ALUM

CHALK

STONE

POTASH

NITER OIL

VINEGAR

BURNED HARTSHORN

URINE

VERDIGRIS

GINGER

MANURE

EGGSHELLS

SUGAR

WINE SPIRIT

YELLOW WAX

HONEY

ROCK SALT

SEA SALT

CINNABAR

PROCESSES

The alchemical process is varied, incorporating solution, evaporation, precipitation, and distillation. The following list of symbols is a sampling of the processes and their symbols.

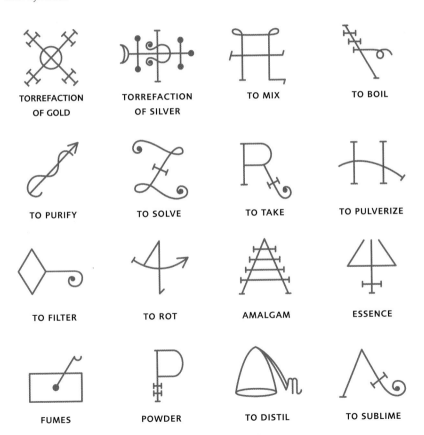

TORREFACTION OF GOLD

TORREFACTION OF SILVER

TO MIX

TO BOIL

TO PURIFY

TO SOLVE

TO TAKE

TO PULVERIZE

TO FILTER

TO ROT

AMALGAM

ESSENCE

FUMES

POWDER

TO DISTIL

TO SUBLIME

INSTRUMENTS

Alchemical substances are put through a series of processes to achieve purification and elevation to "higher" materials. The following symbols represent the instruments used in their transformation.

ALEMBIC

This is the upper part of the still that is used during the process of distillation.

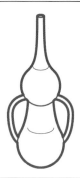

PELICAN

This circulatory vessel with side channels is used to return condensed vapors back to the central cavity. Its name is due to its resemblance to a pelican.

ALUDEL

This pear-shaped earthenware bottle, open at both ends, is used for sublimation, the end-stage of transformation. Other names for the aludel are the hermetic vase and the philosopher's egg.

ATHANOR

Shaped like a structure with a domed roof, this oven is capable of maintaining an even temperature over long periods. It is the alchemical furnace used to perfect matter and burn away impurities. Alchemists called it "house of the chick," in reference to its function as an incubator.

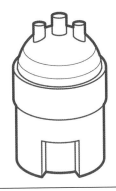

BAIN-MARIE

The bain-marie is a double boiler used to make a warm alchemical bath for the dissolution process. It was named after the Jewish alchemist Maria Prophetissa, who lived in the 3rd century CE. Her alchemical precept, "One becomes two, two becomes three, and out of the third comes the one as the fourth," was used by Carl Jung (see page 12) as a metaphor for the process of wholeness and individuation.

CRUCIBLE

Normally made of porcelain, the crucible is used for melting metals.

WICK

Alchemists use an oil lamp with an asbestos wick to maintain a constant temperature for their work. They regulate the intensity of the heat by choosing the appropriate number of threads used in the wick.

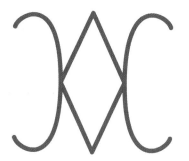

STILL

The distillation process in alchemy involves heating liquid or substances in a still until it vaporizes, enabling its pure extracts to be recovered.

RECEIVER

The receiver is a separate vessel attached to the still that collects the condensed material from the distillation process.

RETORT

A retort is a vessel with a long, tubular neck used in the distillation process. The heated substances evaporate and condense in the neck, enabling the liquid to be collected in a separate receiver vessel.

SKULL

The skull symbolizes mortification, or the end of the first stage of the alchemical Greater Work, in which blackening takes place. Spiritually, it represents dying to the world and the transmutation of the soul to a higher level. The skull also symbolizes the impermanent nature of life.

GRILLE

The grille is a metal screen that provides protection from the intense heat that is generated in some alchemical processes.

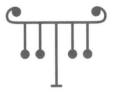

GLASS DROPPER

This dropper is used by alchemists to extract small amounts of liquid.

WEIGHTS

Exact measurement was vital in standardizing alchemical processes. Standard apothecary measures were used to ensure the correct weights of substances and fluids. This system of units of mass was widely used by pharmacists in the English-speaking world before the 19th century.

ONE POUND
This is equal to 12 ounces or 373 grams.

ONE OUNCE
This is equal to 30 grams or 8 drams or 480 grains.

ONE DRAM
Equal to 3.89 grams; a fluid dram equals 3.55 millilitres or 60 minims or 3 scruples.

ONE SCRUPLE
This is equal to 1.296 grams or 20 grains.

ONE PINCH
This is the amount of substance that can be held between the thumb and first finger.

ONE PINT
This is equal to 16 fluid ounces or 0.473 litres.

EQUAL QUANTITY
Alchemists insisted on precise measurements and used exact equal measures in their processes.

GOALS

The best-known goal of the alchemists was the transmutation of base metals into gold or silver. During the Middle Ages, many alchemists came to view material processes as metaphors for transformation on a psychological and spiritual level, ultimately bringing the practitioner to enlightenment.

GOLD

Considered by alchemists the most perfect of metals, gold represents perfection of mind, body, and spirit (see also page 313). It is the archetype or goal of the metallic world, as the golden or perfected human is the archetype or goal of the human realm. Alchemy strives for all metals to be gold and all humans to be pure, enlightened, and incorruptible. It symbolizes evolution from a materialistic world to a spiritual one.

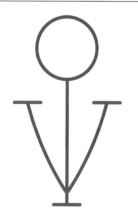

SILVER

Silver is associated with distillation and represents the unsullied nature of the *materia prima*, the primitive formless base of all matter, which manifests in varied forms in the material world. Silver symbolizes lunar, female energy, fertility, and intuition (see also page 315), and its production was associated with the first transformation stage called the Lesser Work. It was combined with the sun, or gold, in the Greater Work, to assure a balance between masculine and feminine.

ASTROLOGY

Since ancient times, humans have watched the skies and observed the movement of the sun, moon, and stars. Knowledge of the skies combined with mythology created the complex system known as astrology. Early astrologers developed intricate systems of glyphs, or symbols, to explain the movement of the sun, moon, and planets through the zodiac. The glyphs shown on pages 202–207 come from medieval manuscripts.

ARIES

Aries (March 21–April 19), the first sign of the zodiac, is a masculine, extroverted sign. A fire sign, it is one of the four cardinal signs representing action (Aries, Cancer, Libra, and Capricorn) and is ruled by the planet Mars (see page 211). In mythology, Aries is associated with Theseus and the Minotaur (see page 48). Those born under Aries take the initiative and perform courageous acts. The symbol of Aries represents the head and horns of a ram and originates from the cluster of stars that make up the "head" of the Aries constellation.

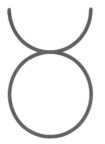

TAURUS

Taurus (April 20–May 20), the second sign of the zodiac, is considered a feminine, introverted sign. An earth sign, it is one of four signs related to stability (Taurus, Leo, Scorpio, and Aquarius) and is ruled by the planet Venus (see page 210). In mythology, it is associated with Aphrodite. Its symbol, which looks like bull's horns, is also one of the alchemical symbols for rock salt. Taureans are grounded, responsible, affectionate, and sensual.

GEMINI

Gemini (May 21–June 21), the third sign of the zodiac, is considered a masculine, extroverted sign. An air sign, it is one of four mutable signs concerned with communication (Gemini, Virgo, Sagittarius, and Pisces) and is ruled by the planet Mercury (see page 210). In mythology, Gemini is associated with the god Hermes/Mercury. Gemini's symbol is the twins and those born under this sign often feel they have a duality of purpose or that they have two separate destinies pulling them in two different directions. Geminis are often known for their open-mindedness and outgoing, inquisitive nature. They are good communicators and multi-taskers.

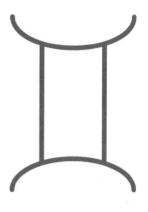

CANCER

Cancer (June 22–July 22), the fourth sign of the zodiac, is considered a feminine, introverted sign. It is also a water sign, one of four cardinal signs, and is ruled by the moon (see page 209). Cancer's symbol is the crab and it is linked with illumination and insight. In mythology, Cancer is associated with the god Hercules. Cancer individuals are known for their sensitive, emotional natures and need their hard shells to retreat into when they become overwhelmed. They are renowned for their nurturing and protective qualities.

LEO

Leo (July 23–August 22), the fifth sign of the zodiac, is a masculine, extroverted sign. A fire sign, it is one of the four fixed signs and is ruled by the sun (see page 208). Its symbol is the lion. Leo individuals are said to have the greatest intensity of the fire signs. In mythology they are associated with the god Apollo. They are less impulsive than Aries individuals and not as prone to wanderlust as those born under a Sagittarius sun. They make excellent leaders, exuding regal authority, and a controlled but powerful presence.

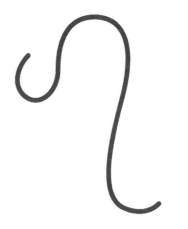

VIRGO

Virgo (August 23–September 22), the sixth sign of the zodiac, is a feminine, introverted sign. It is an earth sign, one of the four mutable signs, and is ruled by the planet Mercury (see page 210). Its symbol is the virgin. In mythology, Virgo is identified with Persephone, daughter of Demeter, the goddess of agriculture. Persephone was the goddess of innocence and purity, but later on became the queen of the underworld, when she was abducted by Hades. Virgo is associated with precision, detail, and transitions.

LIBRA

Libra (September 23–October 23), the seventh sign of the zodiac, is a masculine, extroverted sign. It is an air sign, one of the four cardinal signs, and is ruled by the planet Venus (see page 210). Its symbol is the scales. Libra is often associated with Themis, the Greek goddess of justice (see page 42). Librans love harmony, justice, and equality and they weigh up their choices before taking action. They are diplomatic, fair, idealistic, cooperative, and peace-loving.

SCORPIO

Scorpio (October 24–November 22), the eighth sign of the zodiac, is a feminine, introverted sign. It is a water sign, one of the four fixed signs, and is ruled by the (now ex-) planet Pluto (see page 212). Its symbol is the scorpion. It is associated with birth, death, transformation, sexual relationships, and the occult and psychic matters. In mythology, Scorpio is linked to Hades, ruler of the underworld. Those born under the sign of Scorpio are intense, loving, powerful, secretive, passionate, and loyal.

SAGITTARIUS

Sagittarius (November 23–December 21), the ninth sign of the zodiac, is a masculine, extroverted sign. It is a fire sign, one of the four fixed signs, and is ruled by the planet Jupiter (see page 213). Its symbol is the archer. In mythology, Sagittarius is associated with the centaur Chiron (see page 275) and the Greek god Zeus. Sagittarians are linked with foreign travel, religion, higher education, and whatever expands the mind or experience. They are freedom-loving, adventurous, honest, idealistic, and concerned with morality.

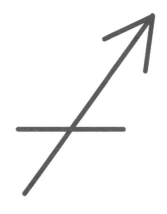

CAPRICORN

Capricorn (December 22–January 19), the tenth sign of the zodiac, is a feminine, introverted sign. It is an earth sign, one of the four cardinal signs, and is ruled by the planet Saturn (see page 212). Its symbol is the goat. In mythology, Capricorn is associated with the gods Saturn and Zeus. Capricorns are known to be practical, disciplined, very methodical, and organized. They can also choose to follow a path to higher spiritual awareness, leaving the material world behind.

AQUARIUS

Aquarius (January 20–February 18), the eleventh sign of the zodiac, is a masculine extroverted sign. It is an air sign, one of the four fixed signs, and is ruled by the planet Uranus (see page 213). Its symbol is the water carrier. In mythology, Aquarius is associated with Odysseus and the Trojan War. Aquarians are known to be strong-willed, magnetic, free-spirited, intelligent, intuitive, idealistic, and somewhat detached emotionally. They can be spontaneous and even erratic, but also inflexible due to their fixed nature.

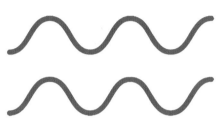

PISCES

Pisces (February 19–March 20), the twelfth sign of the zodiac, is a feminine, introverted sign. It is a water sign, one of the four mutable signs, and is ruled by the planet Neptune (see page 211). Its symbol is a pair of fish swimming in opposite directions, held together by a cord. In mythology, Pisces is associated with the story of Aphrodite and Eros. Pisceans are gentle, good-natured, compassionate, spiritual, impractical, and sometimes naive. They can be dreamy and escapist, but are very likeable.

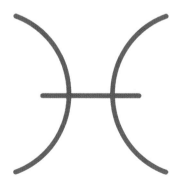

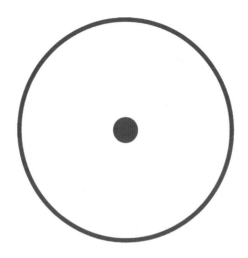

SUN

In astrology, the sun is considered one of the planets. It is the star at the center of our solar system, around which the earth and the other planets revolve. Every day, the sun appears in a slightly different place in the sky, reflecting the earth's changing orbit around it. The sun's arc across the sky is larger at latitudes further north or south from the equator, causing differences in the lengths of days, nights, and seasons. The sun travels through the 12 signs of the zodiac (see pages 202–207) each year and its position on a person's birthday determines his or her sun sign. In Western mythology, the deity of the sun is Apollo.

Astrologically, the sun symbolizes the conscious ego, the self, and its expression. It is yang (see page 146), masculine, paternal, and represents life force. The sun is linked to qualities such as power, assertiveness, pride, authority, leadership, spontaneity, health, and vitality. Most importantly, the quality of a person's creative expression, from parenting to work, has its origin in his or her sun sign.

MOON

The sun sign in which your moon is present when you are born is known as your moon sign and the characteristics of that sun sign affect your moon's expression. Astrologically, the moon is associated with the emotions, the unconscious, memories, changing moods, and the ability to react and adapt to other people and a range of different environments.

While the sun rules your individuality, the moon rules the deeper aspects of your personality, including its hidden aspects. The moon is yin (see page 146), feminine, maternal, receptive, and represents the need for security. It is associated with the breasts and the ovaries in women and with their monthly menstruation.

The moon's gravity has a powerful effect on the earth, stabilizing its orbit and causing the ebb and flow of the tides. The moon is known for its different phases, waxing and waning as it orbits the earth in about 28 days.

In mythology, Artemis, the twin sister of Apollo, represents the moon. Artemis is the goddess of the hunt and also the defender of wild animals and children. The goddess is often depicted with a crescent moon on her forehead and carrying her bow and arrows.

MERCURY

Mercury is the ruling planet of Gemini and Virgo (see pages 203 and 204). In mythology, Mercury was the speedy messenger of the gods and the planet Mercury—equally speedy—takes only 88 days to orbit the sun. In astrology, Mercury represents communication, rationality, reasoning, and adaptability. It is the planet of education, neighbors, siblings, cousins, and messages of all kinds. Mercury is also linked to newspapers, journalism, writing, the Internet, and information-gathering in general.

VENUS

Venus is the ruling planet of Taurus and Libra (see pages 202 and 205) and the second-brightest object in the night sky after the moon. In Roman mythology, Venus was the goddess of love and beauty. The planet Venus orbits the sun in 225 days. Astrologically, Venus represents harmony, beauty, feeling, affections, and the desire to merge with others. It symbolizes pleasure, sensuality, romance, sex, marriage, and partnerships of all kinds. When Venus is in Taurus it is expressed through the physical senses, while in Libra it is expressed as an intellectual sense of harmony and balance.

MARS

Mars is the ruling planet of Aries (see page 202). Before the discovery of Pluto, Mars was also considered the ruler of Scorpio. Mars was the violent Roman god of war. The planet Mars orbits the sun in 687 days. Astrologically, it is associated with masculinity, confidence, ego, energy, passion, drive, aggression, sexuality, strength, ambition, and competition. Its energy can be constructive or destructive. so it is important to harness its forces for good. Stamina, ambition, and achievement can be its positive expressions.

NEPTUNE

Neptune is the ruling planet of Pisces (see page 207). In Roman mythology, Neptune was the god of the sea. Discovered in 1846, the planet Neptune takes 165 years to orbit the sun. In astrology, Neptune is associated with idealism, compassion, spirituality, mysticism, imagination, psychic phenomena, and altered states of consciousness; and, in its negative aspect, with confusion, deception, and drugs and alcohol. Neptune rules the world of illusion—film, TV, theater, and fashion. It invites individuals under its influence to deepen their spirituality in a positive way, through trance, music, or dance.

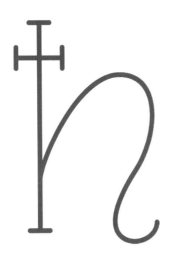

SATURN

Saturn is the ruling planet of Capricorn (see page 206) and, before the discovery of Uranus, of Aquarius. Saturn was the Roman god of agriculture and civilization. The planet Saturn takes 29.5 years to orbit the sun. Astrologically, Saturn is associated with limitation, restrictions, boundaries, practicality, reality, and long-term planning. Discipline and responsibility are central to Saturn. The return of Saturn, about every 30 years, is said to mark significant changes in each person's life. Saturn reminds us of the limitations of time and the need to manage it well.

PLUTO

Pluto is the ruling planet of Scorpio (see page 205). In Roman mythology, Pluto was the god of the underworld and of wealth. The planet Pluto takes 248 years to orbit the sun. Astrologically, Pluto is associated with destruction that ushers in renewal and transformation. It is linked with power, personal mastery, the depths of the unconscious, the collective, and what is hidden from view. In its negative aspect, it governs crime, corruption, obsession, coercion, terrorism, and dictatorships. In its positive aspect, Pluto supports transcendence, redemption, and rebirth.

JUPITER

Jupiter is the ruling planet of Sagittarius (see page 206) and, before the discovery of Neptune, also the ruler of Pisces. In Roman mythology, Jupiter was the ruler of the gods and his symbol was the thunderbolt. The giant planet Jupiter takes 11.9 years to orbit the sun. In astrology, Jupiter is linked to growth, expansion, prosperity, good fortune, leisure, wealth, religion, philosophy, long-distance travel, and higher goals. Although it can feel judgemental, Jupiter is more often a benevolent planet that wants individuals under its influence to grow and flourish.

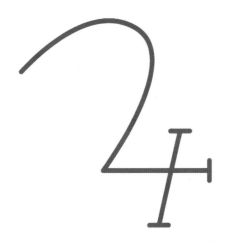

URANUS

Uranus is the ruling planet of Aquarius (see page 207). In Greek mythology, Uranus was the personification of the sky who made love to Gaia, the earth. As the planet Uranus rotates on its side, it stands for the unconventional. Uranus takes 84 years to orbit the sun. Having no use for tradition or the status quo, it sides with genius, individuality, unconventional ideas, computers, cutting-edge technology, new discoveries and inventions, and freedom of expression. Uranus supports humanitarian ideals, equality, freedom, creativity, and political rebellions and revolutions.

THE MOON'S NODES

The moon's nodes are the two points in its orbit that intercept the earth's path around the sun. Node signs are always opposite one another in the zodiac wheel and always appear in pairs. The north node is known as the Dragon's Head and the south node as the Dragon's Tail. In astrology, nodes are significant because they indicate one's capacity for personal and spiritual growth.

The ascending north node produces positive influences and indicates the path of the moon moving from south to north. It represents the future, the direction in which an individual's life is heading, and the lessons that he or she needs to learn. The descending south node marks the intersection of the moon traveling from north to south. It is associated with negative, hindering influences. It represents the past and indicates issues from former lives that need to be addressed.

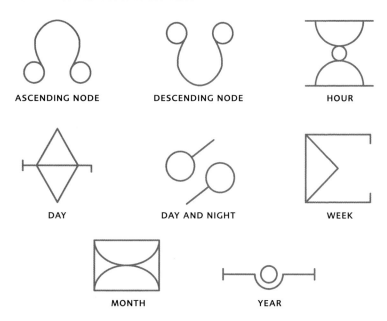

ASCENDING NODE   DESCENDING NODE   HOUR

DAY   DAY AND NIGHT   WEEK

MONTH   YEAR

ASPECTS

These are key to the interpretation of an astrological chart. Aspects are the angles between two or more planets that may be in the sky at the time of one's birth and considering them helps to determine the meaning of those planetary relationships. The major aspects are conjunctions (0 degrees apart or planets right next to each other), sextiles (60 degrees apart), squares (90 degrees apart), trines (120 degrees apart), and oppositions (180 degrees apart). Squares and oppositions are called hard aspects and represent challenges to be overcome. Sextiles and trines are called soft aspects and are considered to be beneficial. Conjunctions can be either positive or negative, depending on the planets involved.

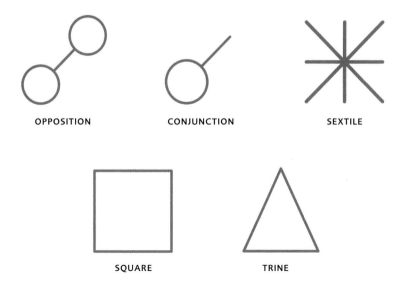

OPPOSITION   CONJUNCTION   SEXTILE

SQUARE   TRINE

CEREMONIAL MAGIC

Ceremonial magic enjoyed a renewed popularity after the practitioner Aleister Crowley (1875–1947) created his own system of occult magic. He emphasized the development of personal power and will, and the practice of conjuring up spirits or entities to assist the magician. He devised complex rituals for focusing the mind to allow the magic to take place and to protect the magician from the conjured entity. Purification practices and the donning of ceremonial robes preceded the ritual. Numerous symbolic and magical objects are used in the production of ceremonial magic.

THE MAGICAL SEALS OF THE SEVEN ANGELS OF THE SEVEN DAYS OF THE WEEK

During the Middle Ages magicians would conjure up spirits, who would then do whatever the magician wanted them to do. The magician would perform the summoning ritual within a magic circle to protect himself from the malevolence of the spirit. Clothing and tools were inscribed with Words of Power, or seals, which contained the names of angels and archangels that were known only to the magician. The day the ritual was performed determined which seal was used.

Michael.

Machen

MICHAEL (SUNDAY)

Gabriel.

Shamain.

GABRIEL (MONDAY)

Samael..

Machon.

SAMAEL (TUESDAY)

Raphael.

Raquie.

RAPHAEL (WEDNESDAY)

Sachiel.

Zebul.

SACHIEL (THURSDAY)

Anael.

Sagun.

ANAEL (FRIDAY)

Cassiel

CASSIEL (SATURDAY)

CEREMONIAL MARKINGS

During ceremonies, magicians would mark their clothing and tools, such as wands and knives, with protective signs and symbols. Each item of clothing or tool had its own seal.

SYMBOLS FOR MARKING THE MAGICIAN'S ROBES

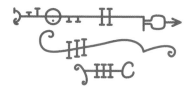

**SYMBOLS FOR MARKING THE
ASSISTANTS' GARMENTS**

SYMBOLS FOR MARKING THE ASSISTANTS' CROWNS

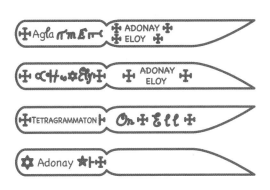

SYMBOLS FOR MARKING THE SWORD

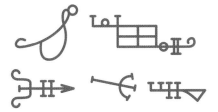

SYMBOLS FOR MARKING THE SHOES

SYMBOLS FOR MARKING THE KNIFE WITH A WHITE HILT

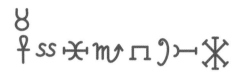

SYMBOLS FOR MARKING THE KNIFE WITH A BLACK HILT

SYMBOLS FOR MARKING THE SCIMITAR

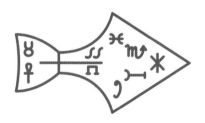

SYMBOLS FOR MARKING THE SHORT LANCE

SYMBOLS FOR MARKING THE DAGGER AND PONIARD

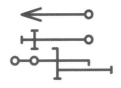

SYMBOLS FOR MARKING THE BURIN

SYMBOLS FOR MARKING THE BELL

SYMBOLS FOR MARKING THE WAND AND STAFF

SYMBOLS FOR MARKING THE TRUMPET

SYMBOLS FOR MARKING THE SILKEN CLOTH

SYMBOLS FOR MARKING THE VIRGIN PARCHMENT

✚ TETRAGRAMMATON ✚ JEHOVA ✚

SYMBOLS FOR MARKING THE NECROMANTIC TRIDENT

SYMBOLS FOR MARKING THE BATON

SYMBOLS FOR MARKING THE BAGUETTE

SYMBOLS FOR MARKING A MAGIC CANDLE

CHARACTERS OF GOOD SPIRITS

Good spirits bring benevolent energies to the ceremonies and rituals of magicians and witches. Invoked to bring positive forces to assist in the creation of magic, these good spirits include nature and guardian spirits.

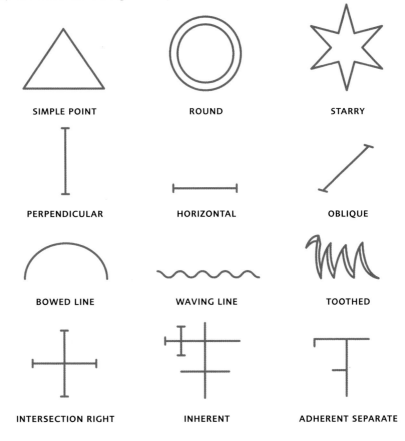

SIMPLE POINT

ROUND

STARRY

PERPENDICULAR

HORIZONTAL

OBLIQUE

BOWED LINE

WAVING LINE

TOOTHED

INTERSECTION RIGHT

INHERENT

ADHERENT SEPARATE

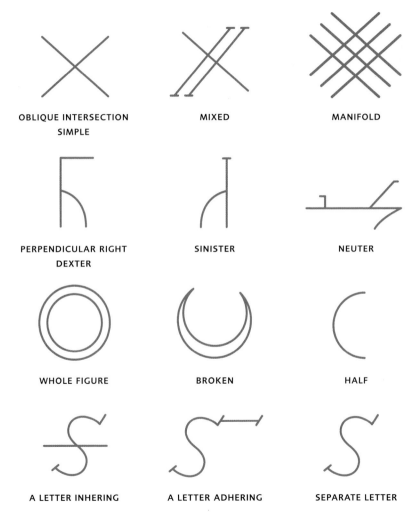

OBLIQUE INTERSECTION SIMPLE

MIXED

MANIFOLD

PERPENDICULAR RIGHT DEXTER

SINISTER

NEUTER

WHOLE FIGURE

BROKEN

HALF

A LETTER INHERING

A LETTER ADHERING

SEPARATE LETTER

CHARACTERS OF EVIL SPIRITS

Evil or malevolent spirits bring destructive forces to magical rituals. In order to ward off these spirits, magicians and witches wear pentangles (see page 96) and inscribe their magical tools with protective words and symbols.

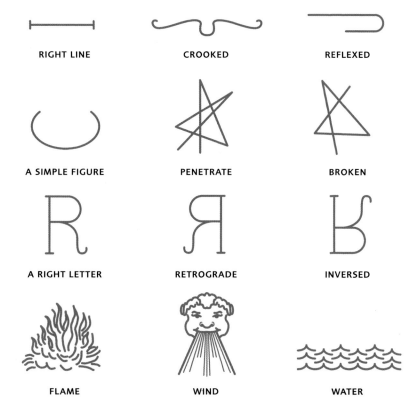

RIGHT LINE

CROOKED

REFLEXED

A SIMPLE FIGURE

PENETRATE

BROKEN

A RIGHT LETTER

RETROGRADE

INVERSED

FLAME

WIND

WATER

FLYING THING

CREEPING THING

SERPENT

EYE

HAND

FOOT

CROWN

CREST

HORNS

SCEPTRE

SWORD

SCOURGE

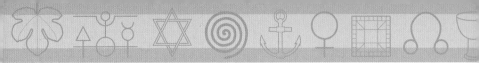

MAGIC SQUARES

Magic squares work by enclosing or trapping an entity or power, by surrounding it with a collection of numbers in a particular relationship. Some magic squares are made up of symbols of planets, metals, or magic words. The numerals and letters that make up the name of God are believed to be especially powerful. One magic square is made up of the Latin sentence *Sator arepo tenet opera rotas*, meaning "The sower at his plough controls the work." In magical squares where the numbers on vertical and horizontal lines always add up to the same number, the result is called the "constant."

4	9	2
3	5	7
8	1	6

SQUARE OF SATURN

4	14	15	1
9	7	6	12
5	11	10	8
16	2	3	13

SQUARE OF JUPITER

11	24	7	20	3
4	12	25	8	16
17	5	13	21	9
10	18	1	14	22
23	6	19	2	15

SQUARE OF MARS

6	32	3	34	35	1
7	11	27	28	8	30
19	14	16	15	23	24
18	20	22	21	17	13
25	29	10	9	26	12
36	5	33	4	2	31

SQUARE OF THE SUN

22	47	16	41	10	35	4
5	23	48	17	42	11	29
30	6	24	49	18	36	12
13	31	7	25	43	19	37
38	14	32	1	26	44	20
21	39	8	33	2	27	45
46	15	40	9	34	3	28

SQUARE OF VENUS

8	58	59	5	4	62	63	1
49	15	14	52	53	11	10	56
41	23	22	44	48	19	18	45
32	34	38	29	25	35	39	28
40	26	27	37	36	30	31	33
17	47	46	20	21	43	42	24
9	55	54	12	13	51	50	16
64	2	3	61	60	6	7	57

SQUARE OF MERCURY

S	A	T	O	R
A	R	E	P	O
T	E	N	E	T
O	P	E	R	A
R	O	T	A	S

SQUARE OF *SATOR AREPO TENET OPERA ROTAS*

37	78	29	70	21	62	13	54	5
6	38	79	30	71	22	63	14	46
47	7	39	80	31	72	23	55	15
16	48	8	40	81	32	64	24	56
57	17	49	9	41	73	33	65	25
26	58	18	50	1	42	74	34	66
67	27	59	10	51	2	43	75	35
36	68	19	60	11	52	3	44	76
77	28	69	20	61	12	53	4	45

SQUARE OF THE MOON

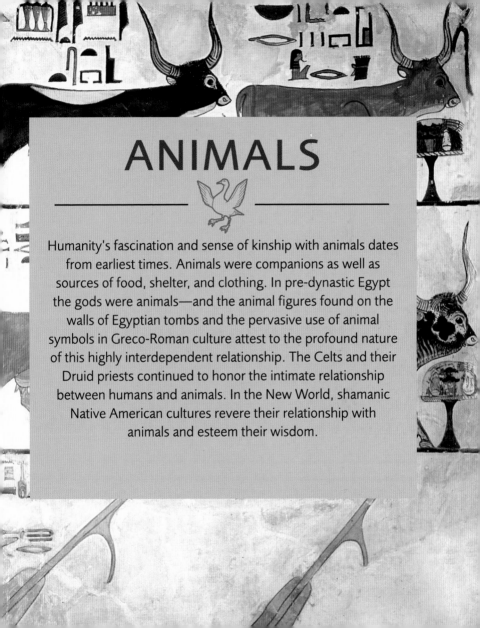

ANIMALS

Humanity's fascination and sense of kinship with animals dates from earliest times. Animals were companions as well as sources of food, shelter, and clothing. In pre-dynastic Egypt the gods were animals—and the animal figures found on the walls of Egyptian tombs and the pervasive use of animal symbols in Greco-Roman culture attest to the profound nature of this highly interdependent relationship. The Celts and their Druid priests continued to honor the intimate relationship between humans and animals. In the New World, shamanic Native American cultures revere their relationship with animals and esteem their wisdom.

MAMMALS

Many Native American creation stories credited animals with the origin of the universe, because animals were considered ancient and humans relatively new to the earth. So it was only natural to turn to animals for knowledge and wisdom. On many totem poles the human figure is found at the bottom rather than at the top, reflecting the human responsibility to honor and care for all other species. Totems were animal mentors and protectors, and each clan or tribe had special relationships with particular animals. Elsewhere, later European and Middle Eastern cultures split animals from humans, with the Hebrews and the Roman Catholic Church forbidding the worship of animals.

BULL

In ancient cultures the Palaeolithic goddess, the Venus of Laussel, is shown holding a crescent-shaped bull horn, while the Egyptian god Osiris was often depicted with the head of a bull. The bull is both a solar and a lunar creature. His male fertility and his fiery temperament make him the masculine sun god in many ancient cultures. However, the bull's crescent-shaped horns link him to moon worship. The moon goddess Astarte often rode a bull. The bull represents valor, bravery, generosity, strength, and fortitude.

COW

Nut, the Egyptian goddess of the night sky, was often represented as a cow, as was the Egyptian goddess Hathor. In many cultures the cow represents the Great Mother, the earth, love, nurturing, warmth, and abundance. Cow deities, such as Nandini, the wish-fulfilling cow, are popular in Vedic literature. In Hinduism, the cow is believed to be a treasure produced from the cosmic ocean by the gods. Because cows are still considered sacred in India today, they are given the freedom to wander wherever they choose. Their horns are often decorated with flowers and colored ornaments, as a sign of respect and affection. The East African Maasai people also consider their cows as gifts from God. According to Norse creation myths, the cow Adumla was the first creature to emerge, and created the first man by licking him out of a salt block.

BUFFALO

At 2,000 lb (900 kg) and 6 feet (1.8 meters) tall at its humped shoulders, the American buffalo, or bison, is an impressive animal. Before every hunt, Native Americans praised the buffalo with a tribal ritual dance. This animal supplied virtually all that the Plains people needed: food, clothing, tools, and housing materials. The animals were called "buffalo people" by some tribes and revered for their power and the good fortune they brought. The hide of the rare white buffalo became a sacred talisman and a priceless possession.

DOG

The dog, the emblem of faithfulness and guardianship, has been one of the most widely kept working and companion animals in human history. Dogs embody courage, playfulness, sociability, and intelligence, and possess excellent hunting skills. The Talbot, an English hunting dog, was found on the coats of arms of famous hunting families. In 13th-century France a greyhound was revered as St. Guinefort. The Greco-Romans, who described those from elsewhere as "dog-headed" peoples, depicted St. Christopher, who was an outsider from the tribe of the Marmaritae, with the head of a dog.

CAT

Cats are inscrutable, nocturnal creatures. The ancient Egyptians and the early Christians revered the cat, but they were persecuted as the familiars of so-called witches during the Middle Ages and became anathema to the Church. They symbolize independence, and the merging of the spiritual with the physical and of the psychic with the sensual. Cats represent wisdom and manifest confidence and self-assurance when confronted. They reach the height of their powers at night and are associated with the moon.

RABBIT

In fairy tales the rabbit appears as the trickster archetype, using its cunning to outwit enemies. The rabbit can also symbolize fertility, innocence, and youthfulness. In China and Japan it is associated with the moon, because the dark areas toward the top of the full moon suggest the form of a rabbit. In China, figures of white rabbits are made for the Moon Festival. In North American folklore, a rabbit's foot is carried as a charm on key chains for good luck (see page 343).

PIG

In many cultures the pig is a fertility symbol, but also represents negative qualities such as gluttony, greed, lust, anger, and the unclean. In some traditions, the sow is associated with the Great Mother. Swine were sacrificed at harvest time to Ceres and Demeter in ancient Greece, in their form as fertility goddesses. In Tibetan Buddhism, the Diamond or Adamantine Sow is Vajravarahi, Queen of Heaven. In Catholicism, St. Anthony is the patron saint of swineherds.

GOAT/RAM

In Egypt, the goat was a symbol of nobility. The horned goat god Pan was one of the oldest Greek deities, associated with nature and sexual energy. Christianity has depicted Satan as having the body parts and horns of a goat, possibly because in the Middle Ages the symbol of lust was a buck in rut. In Chinese astrology, the goat is associated with shyness, introversion, creativity, and perfectionism. In fairy tales and folklore, fauns and satyrs (see page 274) are mythological creatures that are part ram or goat and part human.

SHEEP

The female sheep was associated with the Celtic goddess Brigit or Brighid and her spring festival Imbolic, meaning "ewe's milk." Christ carrying a lamb or a sheep on his shoulders symbolizes the soul of the deceased being borne by him into heaven. Sheep represent the flock or congregation of Christ, who is known as the Good Shepherd. Christ is also portrayed as the Sacrificial Lamb of God or *Agnus Dei* (see page 81). In the Abrahamic faiths, Abraham, Isaac, Jacob, Moses, and King David were all shepherds. In Chinese folklore, because of the way a lamb dances around its mother, it is a symbol of respect and love for parents. Sheep are key symbols in fables and nursery rhymes such as "The Wolf in Sheep's Clothing" and "Baa Baa Black Sheep." In Europe, a black sheep is considered a sign of good luck. In the English language, calling someone a sheep suggests that they are timid and easily led.

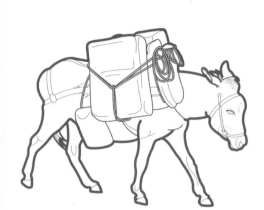

ASS/DONKEY

Asses and donkeys have accompanied humans as pack animals and companions since around 6000 BCE. The ass was a symbol of the Greek wine god Dionysus, the Egyptian god Ra, and Jesus Christ. Asses and donkeys have a reputation for stubbornness, but this is a result of their sense of self-preservation and their own best interests. They are highly intelligent, cautious, friendly, playful, and eager to learn. Folk tales tell of the donkey hiding in various disguises, but giving itself away with its loud braying.

HORSE

Horses personify freedom, sexuality, power, ambition, spirituality, transition, and strength in groups. In Greek myth, Pegasus, the winged horse, was born from the blood of the snake-haired goddess Medusa (see page 46). In Celtic myth, white horses are associated with the goddesses Rhiannon and Epona. In Greek mythology, a centaur is half man and half horse (see page 275). The centaur Chiron was rejected at birth by his human mother, but later became a great compassionate healer. In medical studies, horses have been recognized for their healing effect on humans.

ELEPHANT

There are two species of elephants: the African and the Asian. "Elephant" has its origins in the Greek word meaning "ivory." Elephants are the largest land animals, with the largest brains. They are capable of expressing grief, using tools, showing compassion, and demonstrating self-awareness. Because of their abilities, elephants are a symbol of wisdom in Asian cultures, where they are admired for their memory and high intelligence. Aristotle praised elephants as the animal that surpassed all others in wit and mind.

DEER

Known for its endurance, grace, and long life, the deer is a Chinese symbol for longevity. In Palaeolithic cave paintings at Trois-Frères in France, the figure of a shaman known as The Sorcerer wears antlers embodying the deer-spirit. Many ancient cultures identified the deer with rebirth, because it annually sheds and regrows its antlers. Stags were associated with Cernunnos, the Celtic horned god of nature and hunting (see page 54). Deer are represented in heraldry by the stag or hart.

LEOPARD

The leopard is an agile and stealthy predator. Known as one of the most capricious of the big cats, it is fitting that it draws the chariot of the wine-loving Greek god Dionysus. A ubiquitous African symbol of royal power, the leopard appears on the coats of arms of several African nations, including Benin, Malawi, Somalia, and the Democratic Republic of the Congo. Because it is the only cat known to hunt for pleasure rather than hunger, the leopard symbolizes the dangers and dark side of power.

LION

Although dangerous to humans in the wild, lions are considered strong but gentle. Often called the King of Beasts, the lion is a popular symbol of royalty. One of the key animals in heraldry, it is associated with courage, majesty, and prowess. Mark the Evangelist, the author of the second Gospel, is symbolized by a lion. Although lions are not native to China, the Chinese celebrate the New Year with the Lion Dance to scare away demons and ghosts. In ancient Egypt, the goddess Sekhmet was depicted as a fierce lioness.

WOLF

Human traits assigned to wolves include intelligence, cunning, sociability, and compassion. In the Christian tradition, the wolf represents the devil as the spoiler of the flock. In Roman mythology, a she-wolf suckled Romulus and Remus, the founders of Rome. The wolf was sacred to Mars, god of war. In Japan, grain farmers once worshipped wolves by leaving food offerings near their dens, praying to them to protect their crops from wild boars and deer. For the Aztecs, a howling wolf symbolized Xochipilli, god of dance.

TIGER

In eastern Asia, the tiger represents royalty, fearlessness, and wrath. Its forehead markings resemble the Chinese character for "king." In imperial China, a tiger symbolized war and represented the highest-ranking general. The Chinese god of wealth, Tsai Shen Yeh, rides a ferocious tiger to guard his money chests. The Hindu goddess Durga also rides a tigress into battle. In Tibetan Buddhism, the tiger symbolizes unconditional confidence, disciplined awareness, kindness, and modesty. Relaxed yet energized, it represents the state of enlightenment.

COYOTE

The coyote is revered and feared by Native Americans. He can provide the knowledge and tools for survival, but is also volatile and unreliable. He is a shape-shifter, a trickster, and a transformer. For Native Americans, the coyote is important as a mythological creature rather than as a real animal, and represents the First People, a mythic race who populated the world before humans. They had super-powers and created everything in the world, but were, like humans, capable of both bravery and cowardice, wisdom and stupidity.

FOX

As an animal that roams at the transition times of dawn and dusk, the fox represents shape-shifting and the fairy realms. Foxes charm their prey by twirling around and acting stupidly, until the animal draws within striking distance. Because of their method of hunting, foxes came to be known for their slyness and cunning. The Japanese revered them as the divine messengers of Uka no Mitama, the Shinto rice goddess. Because of their craftiness, beauty, and solitary nature, foxes appeared frequently in Aesop's Fables.

JACKAL

Anubis, the ancient Egyptian god of embalming and the underworld, was depicted as a man with a jackal's head. The jackal, whose opportunistic diet includes carrion, can find a dead body in the open desert, as Anubis guides the dead along their journey in the pathless underworld. The Hindu goddess Durga is often linked with the jackal. The name of Shiva (see page 116) means "jackal" as he is the consort of Kali (see page 118), the destroyer aspect of the Great Goddess. The jackal is also known as a trickster.

BEAR

The bear represents strength, cunning, and ferocity in protection of its family and is a favorite animal on coats of arms. Bears are associated with crystals that are found deep in the caves where they hibernate. Crystals heal through resonance and vibration and by means of the realignment of subtle energies. The bear, the largest of carnivores, is associated with the goddess Artemis-Diana and with the lunar cycle. The Berserkers were ancient Nordic warriors who wore bear shirts into battle, hoping to embody the bear's immense fighting abilities.

MONKEY

One of the most popular Hindu deities is Hanuman, the monkey god known for his courage, perseverance, selflessness, and devotion (see page 122). In the Chinese zodiac, people born in the year of the monkey are often inventors, entertainers, and the creative geniuses behind any undertaking. In general, the monkey symbolizes intelligence and the ability to solve problems. Today, capuchin monkeys are being trained from birth as service animals for those with serious spinal injuries, performing tasks such as opening bottles and putting food in a microwave.

BABOON

The baboon had several manifestations in Egyptian mythology. The baboon god Baba was worshipped in pre-dynastic times and may be the origin of the animal's name. The baboon was also considered sacred as one of the manifestations of Thoth, the god of writing and "one who thinks well." It was considered a protector, inspirer, and an important guide of the writing profession. The baboon was also a magician, skilled at reading all sorts of signs. Not surprisingly, a team of psychologists has recently found evidence of abstract thought in baboons.

BADGER

When defending its home, the badger is remarkably fierce and protective. Because it symbolizes bravery and courage under attack, it is used widely on European coats of arms. Its skill at digging has led to folk beliefs that its paws give good luck in childbirth. The Pueblo consider the badger to be a great healer. Other Native Americans revere it as a storyteller and a keeper of history, legend, and lore. The badger is the power animal of medicine women and the keeper of medicinal roots.

BEAVER

Capa the beaver is an animistic spirit of the Lakota tribe. He is regarded as the patron of hard work and domestic tranquillity. In European heraldry, the beaver represents protection and dedication. It is also known for its industry and perseverance, vigilance, and self-sacrifice, and is an emblem of cooperation and community. In Christianity, the beaver symbolizes chastity. The American beaver is the national animal of Canada and is depicted on the Canadian five cent piece; it also featured on the first postage stamp issued in the Canadian colonies in 1849.

MOUSE

In ancient Greece and Rome, mice symbolized negative qualities such as avarice, greed, and thievery because of their destruction of grain stores. In Hindu lore, the deity Ganesha (see page 121) rides a mouse, as a symbol of intelligence and the ability to penetrate all obstacles. In many cultures the human soul is thought to leave the body in the shape of a mouse at death or while dreaming. In Africa, diviners use mice to determine fortunes. Because mice live so near the ground, they are believed to have a close relationship with earth spirits and ancestors.

RAT

The rat is associated with aggression, death, war, plague, and pestilence. However, the attributes of the Chinese astrological sign of the rat are overwhelmingly positive. Rats are viewed as industrious and clever and the Year of the Rat is considered one of fortune and prosperity. For Hindus, the rat represents prudence and foresight, because rats can be seen leaving a ship before it sinks. To the ancient Egyptians, rats symbolized wisdom. In Japan, a white rat is the symbol of Daikoku, the god of prosperity.

BAT

The bat represents rebirth, transition, and initiation, and night is the bat's time of power. The bat is sacred in Tonga, West Africa, Australia, and Bosnia, and it is often considered the physical manifestation of a soul. It was also sacred to the Aztec, Toltec, and Mayan people as a symbol of rebirth and initiation. In China, the bat was associated with Show-Hsing, the god of longevity. In folklore, bats are closely associated with vampires, who are said to be able to transform themselves into bats. Among some Native Americans, the bat is a trickster spirit. In Poland and Macedonia, the bat is a symbol of good luck. In Japan, the bat symbolizes chaos, unrest, and unhappiness. In Native American cultures, the bat is often the totem of the shaman, who teaches people to go into the night of inner darkness and emerge reborn.

INSECTS

Insects have many symbolic meanings, their behavior suggesting human virtues such as tenacity, patience, and adaptability. One of the first-known insect gods was the scarab beetle worshipped as Khepri, the Egyptian god of the sun.

BUTTERFLY

The fragile short-lived butterfly symbolizes human frailty and the ephemeral nature of life. For Christians, the stages of caterpillar, pupa, and winged adult symbolize spiritual transformation. For the Aztec and Maya, the butterfly was the symbol of the god of fire, Xiutecutli, as fire transforms both food and metal. For Canadian native tribes, the butterfly is associated with the trickster because of its unpredictable flight.

MOTH

The nocturnal moth symbolizes dreams, otherworldliness, and psychic awareness. It is a symbol of the soul yearning for the divine and consumed by mystical love, as the moth is attracted to the candle flame and burns its wings. On a mundane level, a moth burning its wings may be seen as a symbol of frivolity and stupidity. The moth can also represent the human condition, as stated in the Sanskrit text, the *Bhagavad Gita*: "Men rush to their doom like moths flying to their death in the candle flame."

DRAGONFLY

In old Europe, the dragonfly was seen as sinister and was linked to evil and misfortune. In Swedish folk tales, dragonflies were used by the devil to weigh people's souls. The Norwegians called them "eye pokers," while the Dutch called them "horse biters." On the other hand, for Native Americans dragonflies represent the positive qualities of swiftness and activity. They are said to symbolize renewal after periods of hardship. In Japan, dragonflies are symbols of courage, strength, and happiness. The Vietnamese forecast rain by the height at which dragonflies fly.

FLY

In mythology, flies represent evil, death, and decay—as in the fourth of the ten plagues of Egypt in the Bible. Or they represent nuisances—as when the Greek god Myiagros was charged with chasing flies away during sacrifices to Zeus and Athena. In some fables, like the one about the fly on the coach wheel, the fly symbolizes an ineffectual and annoying person. However, in the traditional Navajo religion, Big Fly is an important spirit being, who acts as a mentor and advice-giver, especially to men.

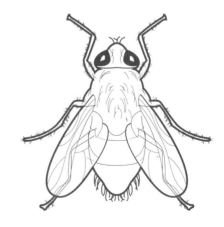

CICADA

For Buddhists, the cicada symbolizes rebirth, as humans shed their bodies the way cicadas shed their skin. Because the ancient Chinese observed cicadas emerge from full-grown but seemingly dead nymphs, they placed cicada-shaped funeral jades on the tongues of the dead to ensure immortality. The cicada symbolizes the Greek god Tithonus, lover of Eos, goddess of the dawn, who asked Zeus to make Tithonus immortal, but forgot to request that he remain youthful. He lived for ever, but became so old that he was transformed into a cicada.

CRICKET

In ancient Chinese culture, crickets were appreciated for their singing, their vitality, and their fascinating life cycles. Because crickets are able to lay hundreds of eggs, people would bless their friends to have as many children as the cricket. But because most crickets sing in the autumn and die with the coming of winter, in poetry they were a symbol of loneliness, sadness, and sympathy for the fate of all humans. Crickets were kept in small cages as symbols of good luck and virtue, near windows so that their song could be enjoyed at night.

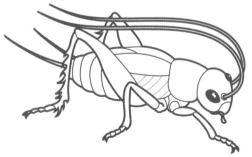

LOCUST

A devouring swarm of locusts represents a destructive scourge or a hellish invasion. Locusts can symbolize spiritual, psychological, or moral torment, or hell-born torments requiring exorcism. In Exodus, one of the plagues of Egypt was a swarm of locusts. In agriculturally rich Egypt, people wore amulets inscribed with the image of a locust to ward off destructive swarms and they also used the locust as a metaphor. On a wall in the temple near modern-day Luxor an inscription reads: "Battalions will come like the locusts."

BEE

In many cultures bees have been thought of as messengers of the spirits. In Celtic lore they represent the wisdom of the other world. In the ancient world, bees represented the soul and, when carved on tombs, symbolized immortality (see also page 43). On ancient coins from the city of Ephesus, a queen bee appears as a symbol of the Great Mother. The Roman god of love, Cupid, is often pictured with bees or being stung. During the medieval period monasteries were centers of bee-keeping and so in Christianity the bee came to symbolize industry, fidelity, and virginity.

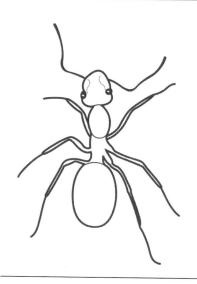

ANT

Ants symbolize strength, hard work, and supportive social structures. Fables and children's stories, such as Aesop's "The Grasshopper and the Ant," represent industriousness and cooperative effort. In the Book of Proverbs in the Bible, humans are exhorted to emulate ants. In some African cultures, ants are considered to be messengers of the gods. In Native American Hopi mythology, they are believed to be the first animals. The Japanese word for ant is the character for insect combined with the character that signifies moral rectitude.

BEETLE

The dung beetle, often referred to as the scarab, was sacred to ancient Egyptians (see page 29). In wall paintings, it pushed the sun along its course in the sky, just as the dung beetle rolls balls of dung to its nest. For Taoists, the scarab's dung ball represented the sacred work necessary to achieve immortality. In South American native mythology, a big scarab beetle named Aksak modeled man and woman from clay. The stag beetle was associated by German artist Albrecht Dürer (1471–1528) with Christ in various paintings.

SCORPION

Scorpions symbolize transitions, death
and dying, sex, control, treachery, and
protection. In the ancient Sumerian poem,
the "Epic of Gilgamesh," Gilgamesh sets
out to descend to the Land of the Dead.
On the way he passes the two mountains
from where the sun rises, which are
guarded by scorpion folk. In Greco-Roman
mythology, Artemis engaged the celestial
scorpion to sting Orion's foot, causing his
death. Scorpio is the eighth sign in the
Western zodiac (see page 205). In the
Christian tradition, a scorpion symbolizes
Judas Iscariot, the epitome of treachery.

SPIDER

The spider represents resourcefulness,
mystery, power, growth, the feminine,
death, rebirth, and fate. Most spiders have
eight eyes and all have eight legs. The
number eight on its side is a lemniscate, or
a symbol of infinity. In Greek mythology,
Arachne was a gifted weaver but arrogant,
and she challenged Athena to a weaving
duel. Insulted by the image of Zeus's
loves that Arachne wove, the goddess
punished her, and Arachne killed herself.
In remorse, Athena resurrected Arachne in
the form of a spider so that she would for
ever be the best weaver of the universe.

BIRDS

From ancient times, in many cultures, birds have functioned as gods, oracles, and messengers. Because of their swift flight and sudden appearance, they are often read as omens of good or ill. Their domain is the air element, so they are considered to be mediators between the earthly and heavenly realms—or the physical and spiritual worlds. As humans observed the flight of birds, it was easy to see them as a symbol of the human soul. In Christianity, birds often signify the presence of God, as in the dove symbolizing the Holy Spirit or the sparrow representing God's concern for the most insignificant living things.

GOOSE

The goose symbolizes migrations and transitions, as well as the hearth and home, as it returns to the same spot every spring. In China and ancient Egypt, geese were regarded as messengers between heaven and earth. When a new pharaoh was proclaimed, four geese were sent out in four directions to announce his arrival. In ancient Rome, geese were kept as guardians of the temple of Juno and would cackle loudly when strangers approached. In the Celtic tradition, geese were messengers from the otherworld and it was forbidden to use them as food.

DUCK

In cultures around the world, the duck attracts much humor and silliness and has inspired many cartoon characters. Because it floats on the surface of the water, the duck symbolizes superficiality, chatter, and deceit. However, the duck can also dive underwater and reappear in a very different location—in colloquial language it has "ducked out." Ducks also symbolize gracefulness and friendliness. In Chinese and Japanese culture, a Mandarin duck and drake pictured together represent marital happiness and fidelity. Ancient Egyptians associated the duck with marshland, a mysterious, dangerous, yet life-giving place.

HEN

The hen symbolizes self-sacrifice, nurturing, protection, and comfort. In the 1st century CE the Roman historian Plutarch praised the hen as using all parts of her body to cherish her chicks—letting down her wings and arching her back for them to climb on. In the Bible, Jesus uses the hen and her sheltering wings to describe Christian love as being like a mother's love for her children. In the Congo, the hen serves as the conductor of the soul in the initiatory rites of female shamans of the Bantu tribes.

COCK

In most cultures, the cock is a solar symbol and a sign of illumination. In the Christian tradition, the cock crowing was said to wake men and women out of their secular sleep into the spiritual world of the Gospel. Cock weathervanes on churches symbolized vigilance against evil. When the cock crowed at dawn, all evil things of the night—ghosts, vampires, and evil spirits—were said to vanish. Because it shares its food with the hen, the cock symbolizes generosity. Because of its bravery, it is associated with the Greek god Ares.

STORK

Because storks are deeply devoted to their offspring, they are symbols of good parenting. For early Christians the stork represented a respected marriage of virgins, but although mistakenly thought to mate for life, in reality storks practice serial monogamy. In rural Denmark, a stork building a nest on a roof means bad luck and suggests that a death will occur in the house within a year. In Bulgarian folklore, the sighting of a stork returning from its winter migration is a sign of spring. Sometimes Western parents tell young children that "a stork brought the baby."

SWAN

The Celts wore images of pairs of swans around their necks for protection. In Hindu culture, the swan signifies the mind of God and a swan is the mount of the goddess Saraswati. In the Ugly Duckling fable by Hans Christian Andersen, a mistreated ugly duckling (in reality a cygnet) grows up to be a breathtakingly beautiful swan. Because swans mate for life, they symbolize love and fidelity. In the Greek myth of Leda and the swan, Helen of Troy was born of the union of Zeus (disguised as a seductive swan) and Leda, Queen of Sparta.

DOVE

The moaning call of the dove is associated with sex and childbirth, but the dove is also a symbol of purity and peace (see page 82). In the Old Testament, Noah sent out a dove to see if the waters had receded and it returned with an olive branch, signifying a truce between God and humans. A dove, as a symbol of a pure soul, is depicted flying from the mouth of martyred Christian saints. When John the Baptist baptized Christ, he saw the Holy Spirit descend like a dove upon him.

LARK

The lark, or skylark, symbolizes the marriage of heaven and earth as it flies swiftly upward and then dives back down to the ground. Its early morning song and flight symbolize youthful enthusiasm, merriment, and the human desire for happiness. It is also the symbol for hope, happiness, good fortune, and creativity. For Christian mystics, the lark's song symbolized a joyful prayer to God. Shakespeare twice refers to the lark "singing at heaven's gate." In *Romeo and Juliet*, the lark symbolizes daybreak.

PEACOCK

The peacock is a favorite bird on many coats of arms, symbolic of personal pride. It is also the bird of the Hindu god Krishna (see page 117), who wears peacock feathers in his hair. Saraswati, the goddess of poetry, music, and wisdom, rides a peacock, and it is associated with the Japanese and Chinese goddesses of mercy, Kannon and Kwan Yin. In Buddhism, the peacock's ability to eat poisonous snakes is a symbol of the transmutation of evil into good. In Islam, peacocks are said to be the greeters at the gates of paradise. In the Christian tradition, the peacock is a symbol of eternity and immortality.

EAGLE

The eagle's wings symbolize protection, and the gripping talons and sharp beak represent the threat of destruction. Many nations and organizations use the eagle on their coats of arms. In Christianity, the eagle symbolizes John the Apostle and its soaring quality stands for the first chapter of his Gospel. The eagle is a sacred bird to many Native American tribes and eagle feathers are central to numerous religious customs and tribal ceremonies. The eagle, as spiritual being and ancestor, sometimes appears on totem poles.

FALCON

The falcon is solar and male, and represents spirit, visionary power, light, freedom, guardianship, and victory. It symbolizes the lifting of spirit, intellect, and morals. The falcon was associated with the rising sun in Egypt. It represented the Egyptian god Horus, who was shown with the head or body of a falcon (see page 25). In European mythology, the falcon was a symbol of war and the hunt and was associated with the Germanic sky gods Wodan and Frigg. For Peruvian Incas, the falcon symbolized the sun.

OWL

The owl signifies wisdom, intelligence, mystery, mysticism, and secrets. In ancient cultures it was considered the ruler of the night, guardian of the underworlds, and protector of the dead. In ancient Greece, the owl was sacred to the goddess Athena. Because of its ability to see at night, the owl was invoked by Native Americans as an oracle of hidden knowledge. In Europe, during medieval times, owls were considered witches and wizards in disguise. In Indian culture, a white owl is a companion of Lakshmi, the goddess of prosperity (see page 119).

RAVEN

In some later Western European traditions, ravens symbolize ill omens, misfortune, and death. In contrast, many indigenous people of North America and northeast Asia revere the raven as a god. In China and Japan, the raven symbolizes filial gratitude and family affection. The raven was also associated in China with the sun. In ancient Greece, the raven was a bird sacred to Apollo, where it acted as a messenger to the gods. For the Likuba tribe of the Congo Basin, the raven provided a warning of dangers.

PARROT

In world mythology, because of their talkativeness, parrots are the messengers between humans and gods. In Indian mythology, the chariot of Kama, god of love, is drawn by a parrot. The parrot is also an emblem for Devi and other female deities. In the European Christian tradition, the parrot was a symbol of the Immaculate Conception, which was considered to have taken place in an exotic country—the bird talking into Mary's ear stood for the Conception taking place through the ear, via the Word of God.

OSTRICH

In mythology, the ostrich is said to hide its head in the sand at the first sign of danger. From this derived the old saying "Don't hide your head in the sand," meaning that one should not ignore a problem, hoping it will go away. Ancient naturalists, noting that the ostrich would eat anything, thought it ate iron and because of this misconception the ostrich is shown in heraldry with a horseshoe in its mouth. In the Book of Job in the Bible, the ostrich also symbolizes a neglectful parent.

PELICAN

During the nesting season some pelicans grow red feathers on their breast and as a result, in medieval Europe, the female pelican was believed to wound her breast with her long, curved bill, drawing blood to feed her young. Because of this misunderstanding, the pelican became a symbol of self-sacrifice and maternal love.

The pelican also became a symbol of the Passion of Jesus Christ and the Eucharist. The emblems of the two Corpus Christi colleges, one at Oxford and the other at Cambridge, is a pelican (*corpus christi* means "Body of Christ"). In heraldry, the pelican is always shown "wounding" or "vulning" itself.

FISH

A symbol of Christianity and Christ, the fish was linked by the pagan cultures of northern Europe to fertility and feminine power. In Indian cultures, it was linked with reincarnation and life force. In ancient Greece, "fish" and "womb" were synonymous and the *esica piscis* (a pointed oval) referred to the Great Mother.

CARP

As the carp swims upstream, the Japanese associate it with perseverance in adversity. The carp, or koi, stands for courage and worldly aspiration and achievement. On Children's Day, the Japanese display carp-shaped kites and windsocks to summon strength and success for their offspring. In Chinese art and literature, a jumping carp symbolizes a leap in social status through promotion or marriage.

SALMON

Irish hero Fionn mac Cumhaill gains his powers of perception from eating the "salmon of knowledge." In Welsh myth, the salmon is the world's oldest animal. In Norse mythology, the trickster god Loki turns into a salmon to escape punishment from the other gods. For Native Americans, the salmon symbolizes rebirth and renewal. As the salmon dies after spawning, it is associated with the spirits of the dead.

CONCH

Conch shells are used as musical wind instruments in Hindu culture and some island cultures. The Sanskrit epic, the *Mahabharata*, describes warriors of ancient India blowing conch shells as they go into battle. The Hindu god Vishnu holds a conch shell named Panchjanya that symbolizes life emerging from water (see page 117). The conch is one of the Eight Auspicious Symbols of Buddhism (see page 134) and symbolizes Buddha's voice preaching the Dharma. It is also a symbol of the Greek god Poseidon and, in Islam, it is the ear that hears the divine Word.

LOBSTER

The lobster, a lunar being, symbolizes cycles, regeneration, and protection. It casts off its shell for a new one and thus represents rebirth. Its hard, external skeleton represents personal protection. As a scavenger, the lobster symbolizes the ability to make use of every aspect of experience. In ancient Peru, the Moche people worshipped sea animals and lobsters appeared frequently in their imagery. In Japanese culture, the lobster represents longevity and happy, celebratory events. It is especially associated with New Year.

OCTOPUS

The octopus symbolizes mystery, flexibility, fluidity, intelligence, adaptability, and unpredictability. It is a lunar creature, affected by the tides and the waxing and waning of the moon. It dwells on the ever-changing bottom of the ocean and, not having a skeleton, can move quickly and escape from the tightest places. It has the capability to detach a limb in order to free itself from a predator. The octopus symbolizes creativity, moving toward goals in unorthodox ways, and the ability to lose excess emotional or physical baggage.

DOLPHIN

Since ancient times humans have been attracted to the dolphin's intelligence, graceful body, effortless movement, human-like eyes, and permanent "smile." In Christianity, because dolphins swam alongside boats, they became a symbol of Christ who guides souls to heaven. In an Inuit legend, a young girl named Sedna refused to marry; when her enraged suitors tried to drown her at sea, she grasped the edge of the boat, but the men chopped off all her fingers. Her severed fingers fell into the ocean and turned into the world's first whales, dolphins, seals, and walruses.

WHALE

The whale represents the tomb and regeneration. In the myth of Jonah and the whale, the swallowing of Jonah by the whale symbolizes the "death" that takes place during spiritual initiation. His ejection from the whale's belly after three days represents the subsequent resurrection and rebirth. In Christianity and some Polynesian myths, passing through the belly of a whale was seen as a descent into hell. In Islamic mythology, God created the whale as a foundation for the cosmos and whenever it moved, it caused earthquakes.

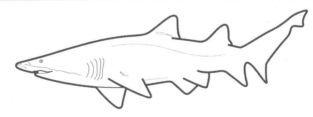

SHARK

The shark is a symbol of the dangers of nature and often represents terror and violence. In Hindu mythology, Vishnu (see page 117) is sometimes portrayed as emerging from the mouth of a shark. Hawaiians believed sharks to be the guardians of the sea and Hawaiian mythology features many shark gods. The best known of these was Kamohoali'I, the brother of the goddess Pele. Ka'ahupahau was a goddess born human with bright-red hair, who was later transformed into a shark in order to protect the people who lived on O'ahu from other sharks.

REPTILES AND AMPHIBIANS

Reptiles and amphibians symbolize cycles, change, duality, and mystery: the snake sheds its skin, the tadpole transforms into a frog, and amphibians are able to exist in two worlds or two environments. In ancient Egyptian and Greek symbolism, the reptile represented divine wisdom and good fortune and was an attribute of Hermes. In Roman mythology, the reptile, which was thought to sleep through the winter, symbolized death and resurrection. Early Christianity associated the lizard with the devil, yet the Polynesians and Maoris revere it as a god. In India, *nagas* are semi-divine beings with serpent bodies.

LIZARD

The lizard symbolizes subtlety, sensitivity, quickness, and intuitive and psychic abilities. It recognizes the subtlest movements in others and can remain virtually motionless to mislead its prey or protect itself. Lizards have long tails that lend balance and they can be detached and regrown as needed. In ancient Egypt and Greece, the lizard symbolized divine wisdom and good fortune. In Roman mythology, lizards were thought to sleep through the winter and therefore represented death and resurrection. In some Native American traditions, the lizard is associated with dreamtime and dreams.

CHAMELEON

A chameleon can change skin color in response to light and temperature, as well as emotions and the presence of a mate. In Christianity, the chameleon symbolizes the devil taking different appearances to deceive and attract humans. Because a chameleon's eyes move independently, chameleon talismans were used in ancient Rome as a cure for blindness. For Sufis, a chameleon symbolized an inconsistent person—one who changed his being to suit the circumstances.

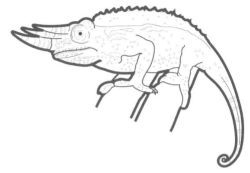

SALAMANDER

Salamanders have a strong symbolic relationship to fire that probably originates in their practice of hibernating in rotting logs. When wood was brought indoors and put on the fire, a salamander magically appeared from the flames. As it exudes a moist, milky substance when frightened, the idea emerged that the salamander could withstand fire. In heraldry, it is depicted surrounded by flames and it became the traditional emblem of the blacksmith. In Christianity, the salamander was a symbol of faith and virtue, which triumphs over the fires of passion.

FROG

In folklore, frogs are powerless and ugly but brimming with undeveloped, hidden talents. Laying many eggs, they symbolize fertility and abundance. In Egypt, Heket is the frog-headed goddess of birthing. In Christianity, the frog's three stages of development—egg, tadpole, and adult amphibian—symbolize spiritual evolution. In Christian art, the frog is a symbol of the Holy Trinity. For the Celtic people, it stood for healing. In China, the frog or toad is an emblem of good luck (see page 345).

ALLIGATOR/CROCODILE

Inhabiting both land and water, alligators and crocodiles (known collectively as crocodilians) represent contradiction and the duality of nature. In ancient Egypt, crocodiles were considered sacred, as well as being feared and reviled. They were also equated with the fertility of the life-giving waters of the Nile. In the city of Crocodopolis, crocodiles were adorned with earrings and fed daily to honor Sobek, the crocodile-headed god. In China, the alligator was thought to have invented singing and the drum. And the *Crocodylus porosus*, an ancient giant crocodile, may be the origin of dragon lore in China. The sensitivity of the crocodile to changes in air pressure and coming rain may have been the source of the dragon's mythical ability to control rain and weather. For Australian Aboriginals, the crocodile is associated with wisdom. In West Africa, the crocodile's liver and entrails are used by shamans to cast maleficent spells.

SNAKE

The snake trying to swallow its tail is a symbol for eternity and life begetting life (see page 89). One of the most complex symbols in the world, the snake symbolizes male and female, death and destruction, life and resurrection, light and darkness, good and evil, healing and poison, wisdom and blind passion. As it sheds its skin, it represents letting go of the past and rebirth. The snake lives in the underworld, or realm of the dead, and represents both the unconscious and transcendence. As a phallic symbol, it represents sexuality and sexual union.

TORTOISE

The tortoise, as representative of the lunar, feminine principle, symbolizes water, the moon, earth goddesses, reproduction, creation, and immortality. In creation myths it is often depicted holding up the world.

For Taoists, the tortoise symbolized the whole universe: its shell stood for the heavens; its body, for humans; its flat base, for the earth. Like the crane, the tortoise is a symbol of longevity. For Hindus, it is an emblem of Vishnu, the preserver (see page 117). For the Japanese, it was a companion of the river goddess Benten, patron of the arts.

MYTHICAL CREATURES

These chimerical creatures are composites of different parts of different beasts, such as the head of one animal and the torso of another, with magical attributes such as dragon wings. Fabulous beasts symbolized the chaos of the real world, where a life could be altered in the blink of an eye. Winged, clawed monsters were popular in heraldry, where they protected the charge.

DRAGON

Dragons appear all over the world, the European and Oriental dragons being the two most familiar examples. Reptilian monsters all possess magical or spiritual qualities. In eastern Asian cultures, dragons are beneficent and symbolize nature's primal forces, supernatural power, wisdom, and strength. In the West, they are often destructive and evil, representing monsters that a hero must fight. They can be male or female and often guard land, portals, or treasures.

WYVERN

A wyvern is a legendary two-legged winged dragon with a serpent's tail, often found in medieval European heraldry. Wyverns symbolize strength, valor, protection, and vision, especially in their role as guardians of clan members and treasure. They also represent power and endurance. The wyvern was associated with the rulers of Wessex in south and southwest England.

CHIMERA

The chimera is a hybrid monster with a lion's head and legs, a goat's body and a snake's or dragon's tail. It may also be shown with three heads, those of a lion, goat, and dragon or snake. The lion's head represents a damaging tendency to dominate. The goat's body represents sexual perversion and promiscuity that harms the body. The snake or dragon's tail symbolizes boastful pride contaminating the spirit. The Greek hero Bellerophon defeated the chimera with the aid of his winged horse, Pegasus. A chimera stands for psychological suffering born of unrestrained imagination.

GRIFFIN

The griffin is a masculine creature with the head, wings, and talons of an eagle and the body of a lion. It first appeared in 2000 BCE in Asia, then later in Greece, where it was sacred to Apollo and represented solar wisdom and power. In the Middle Ages in Europe, it represented Christ's dual nature as man and god. In heraldry, a griffin symbolizes the bearer having the dual strength of the lion and the eagle. A griffin borne on a shield was said to instil fear in the horses of the bearer's opponents.

HIPPOGRIFF

The hippogriff is a legendary creature, born of a griffin (see page 273) and a mare. It has the head, wings, and front legs of a griffin and the hind parts of a horse. This mating was rare, because the griffin considers the horse as prey and so the hippogriff was a symbol of impossible things and unrealizable love. A popular saying in the Middle Ages to express the impossible was "to cross griffins with horses." The hippogriff, being easier to tame than a griffin, became the mount for knights in Charlemagne's legends.

SATYR

Male companions of the Greek god Dionysus and the Roman god Bacchus, satyrs symbolized the sex drive and were often portrayed with an erection. In the Greek tradition they appear with a horse's tail. In the Roman tradition they are frequently described as having the upper half of a man and the lower half of a goat. Satyrs are rogues. They are also subversive, shy, and cowardly, and love wine, women, and boys. They enjoy music and dancing with the nymphs.

CENTAUR

In Greek mythology, the centaur Chiron had the upper body of a man and the lower body of a horse. He was a positive figure, gentle, and wise. He was tutored by Apollo and Artemis and in turn was a mentor to others. Rejected at birth by his human mother, he later became a great compassionate healer. Chiron symbolizes suffering as part of the human condition, and the fact that personal knowledge and the experience of suffering can be useful in helping others who are in pain.

UNICORN

A mythological horse with a lion's tail and the hooves of an antelope, the unicorn is often depicted as white in color with a single horn on its forehead and described as mysteriously beautiful. Its horn was believed to be a powerful antidote against poison. Unlike most mythical creatures, it is good, selfless, magical, pure, and innocent. According to legend, only a virgin could capture a unicorn; it would sense her purity and lay its head in her lap. In Christian iconography, the unicorn symbolizes the Incarnation of Christ as well as chaste love and faithful marriage.

SPHINX

A sphinx has the body of a lion and the head of a human. Similar creatures appear in Egypt, Greece, and south and southeast Asia. In Egypt, the recumbent sphinx guarded the temple or royal tombs—the largest and most famous being the Great Sphinx of Giza. In Greek mythology, the sphinx was a female demon of destruction and bad luck, depicted as a winged lion in a seated position, with a woman's head. She guarded the entrance to the city of Thebes and asked a riddle of travelers who wished to obtain passage. (See also page 39.)

MANTICORE

The manticore has the body of a red lion, the face and ears of a human, and a trumpet-like voice. The mouth contains three rows of teeth and the manticore can shoot out poisoned spines from its tail, paralyzing or killing its victims. The manticore myth originated in Persia, where its name meant "man-eater." The creature enjoyed attacking humans and would challenge them with riddles before killing them. In the Middle Ages the manticore became the symbol of tyranny, disparagement, and evil.

ENFIELD

The enfield is a fictitious heraldic beast with the head of a fox, the chest of a greyhound, the body of a lion, the hindquarters and tail of a wolf, and forelegs like an eagle's claws. The enfield appears in the Book of O'Kellys (1394 CE), a famous ancient manuscript of Ireland. It is said that the chieftain Tadhg Mor O'Kelly fell while fighting the Danes in 1014 CE and the enfield emerged from the nearby sea to protect his dead body until it could be given a proper burial.

HARPY

In Greek mythology, the harpies were winged female death-spirits known for stealing food from Phineas, a king of Thrace who had the gift of prophecy. Because Phineas revealed too much, Zeus punished him by having the harpies steal the food out of his hands before he could eat. Jason and the Argonauts rescued Phineas by driving off the harpies. The harpies also abducted people and tortured them on the way to Tartarus. They were vicious, cruel, and violent and may have been the personifications of the destructive nature of wind.

PHOENIX

The phoenix, a symbol of fire, divinity, and invincibility, is a mythical bird with a tail of beautiful gold and red feathers. The symbol is found in many cultures. When the phoenix has lived for 1,000 years, it builds itself a nest of cinnamon twigs in an oak or palm tree and ignites it with the help of the sun. The phoenix and its nest then burn furiously and are reduced to ashes, from which a new, young phoenix arises. It is said that the new phoenix can regenerate itself when hurt or wounded. In Christian art, the phoenix is a symbol of Christ's resurrection.

BASILISK

The mythological basilisk has the head of a bird and the body of a serpent. It symbolizes lust, disease, and treachery. It has poisonous breath and can kill with a look. In Christian art, it represents the Antichrist or a manifestation of the devil. To Protestants, the basilisk was a symbol of the papacy. Its origin may be the horned or hooded cobra from India. By the Middle Ages, overactive imaginations had made it a snake with the head of a cock. Chaucer wrote of a basilisk in his *Canterbury Tales*.

MERMAID

The mermaid is a mythical aquatic creature with the head and torso of a human female and the tail of an aquatic mammal. The mermaid appears in the folk tales of many cultures throughout the world: the water goddess Mami Wata of west Africa; the merrow of Scotland and Ireland; the rusalkas of Russia; the naiads of Greece. Mermaids may be characterized as seductive, dangerous, or helpful. In Hans Christian Andersen's famous fairy tale, "The Little Mermaid," the mermaid is told that she can only obtain an immortal soul by marrying a human being.

SEA DOG

The sea dog is a fabulous beast in the form of a dog, not unlike the Talbot (an old hunting dog), with a dorsal fin along its back, a scaled body and legs, webbed feet, and a beaver's tail. It is often depicted in a blue or green color. The sea dog symbolizes both sea ports and seasoned sailors. It is a sea chimera, a hybrid monster of the sea like the mermaid.

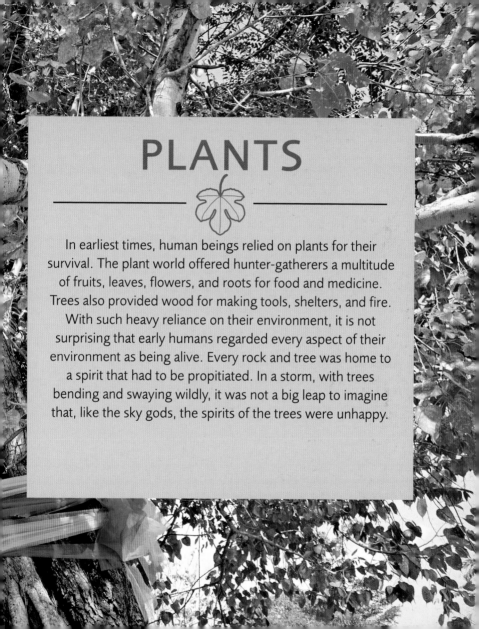

PLANTS

In earliest times, human beings relied on plants for their survival. The plant world offered hunter-gatherers a multitude of fruits, leaves, flowers, and roots for food and medicine. Trees also provided wood for making tools, shelters, and fire. With such heavy reliance on their environment, it is not surprising that early humans regarded every aspect of their environment as being alive. Every rock and tree was home to a spirit that had to be propitiated. In a storm, with trees bending and swaying wildly, it was not a big leap to imagine that, like the sky gods, the spirits of the trees were unhappy.

TREES

Connections between gods and trees were common in classical times. The Greek god Apollo was associated with the laurel, the Egyptian god Osiris with the cedar, and the Greek goddess Athena with olive trees. At Saturnalia, Romans decorated trees with candles and brought evergreens into their homes to honor the tree spirits and the new year. In the Celtic tradition, trees were venerated as a link between heaven and earth. In Scandinavia, the ash tree, known as Yggdrasil, was a symbol of universal life, connecting Midgard (the dwelling place of humans), Asgard (the home of the gods), and Hel (the underworld). Today, belief in the mystical power of trees continues.

OLIVE

The Roman poet Horace (65–8 BCE) mentions the olive as the main part of his simple diet. In his time, olives were considered to be one of the most perfect foods. The olive leaf was a symbol of abundance, glory, and peace, as well as of benediction and purification. It was ritually offered to deities and kings and to the victors of athletic games. The oil from the olive, which was considered sacred, was used in religious ceremonies, burned in lamps in the temples, and used to fuel the "eternal flame" of the original Olympic Games. The olive tree was said to be sacred to the Greek goddess Athena and was her gift to the people of Greece. In gratitude they made her the patron of the city of Athens.

Some olive trees in Italy today are believed to date back to Roman times and several trees in the Garden of Gethsemane in Jerusalem are claimed to date from the time of Jesus. One olive tree in Crete has been verified as being 2,000 years old using tree-ring analysis.

OAK

The oak is a symbol of strength and endurance found in various cultures around the world and is the national tree of many countries, including England, France, Germany, Poland, and the United States. Several individual oak trees, such as the Royal Oak in the English West Midlands and the Charter Oak in Connecticut in the US, are of great historical or cultural importance.

In Celtic mythology, the oak represents doors and gateways between worlds or marks the place where portals to the underworld could be erected. In Norse mythology, the oak was sacred to the thunder god, Thor. It is speculated that this was because oaks—being the largest tree in northern Europe—often drew lightning in a storm. In Greek mythology, the oak was a symbol of Zeus and his sacred tree. The oracle of Dodona, in prehistoric northwestern Greece, consisted of a holy oak; priestesses and priests interpreted the rustling of its leaves to determine the correct actions to be taken.

There are numerous proverbs about the oak as an inspiration for living, such as "Mighty oaks from little acorns grow."

FIG

In the Old Testament, the fig tree was a symbol of prosperity and security. It was from fig trees that Adam and Eve fashioned their first covering. The fig has been used in art throughout the centuries to cover the genitals and as a symbol of chastity. The Bodhi Tree under which the Buddha gained enlightenment (see page 133) is a famous species of fig that is held sacred in India, where it is also a symbol of plenty and immortality. The fig represented spiritual wisdom and Egyptians used the fig in initiation rites.

CEDAR

The cedar tree symbolizes strength and loyalty and is the emblem of Lebanon. It is associated with healing, cleansing, and protection. According to the Old Testament, the Temple of Solomon was built of resinous, scented cedar wood, and the gum of the cedar was also used for embalming. In Sanskrit, the word for cedar means "timber of the gods." Cedar was often found near shrines as it was thought to help reveal the secrets of heaven and drive away malevolent spirits.

LAUREL

In the Bible, the laurel is associated with fame and prosperity. It symbolizes the resurrection of Christ and the saving of humanity. In Greek mythology, the laurel tree came into being when the nymph Daphne's father transformed her into one so that she could escape the lustful advances of Apollo. Apollo took the laurel as his symbol and *dhafni* became the Greek name for the laurel tree (see page 42). According to Chinese folklore, there is a laurel tree on the moon; in Chinese, the name for laurel means "moon-laurel."

HAWTHORN

The hawthorn tree, a sacred tree of Wicca and witchcraft, is associated with Beltane or May Day, the spring celebration that honors the sun god Belenus. In Irish folklore, cutting the hawthorn was considered bad luck because the fairies inhabiting it might be offended. In Germanic lore, the hawthorn is a symbol of death and its wood is used on funeral pyres. In Greece, wedding couples traditionally wore crowns of hawthorn blossom. Cardea, the Roman goddess of marriage and childbirth, was associated with the hawthorn.

HAZEL

The hazel tree symbolizes hidden wisdom, dousing, and divination. In mythology, the hazel functions as a container of ancient wisdom and eating its nuts is said to bring about heightened spiritual awareness. In the Celtic legend of Fionn mac Cumhaill, he gains wisdom by eating a salmon (see page 264) that fed on hazelnuts. (Interestingly, contemporary scientific studies have shown the hazelnut to be excellent nourishment for brain function.) In Ireland today, a forked hazel branch continues to be used for divining water.

JUNIPER

The juniper tree is associated with warding off illness, negative forces, and evil. It was burned in ancient Sumeria and Babylonia as a sacrifice to the gods and was sacred to the goddesses Inanna and Ishtar (see page 34). Fleeing to Egypt with the infant Jesus, Mary and Joseph hid behind a juniper tree to avoid King Herod's soldiers. In Europe, smouldering juniper branches were carried around fields to protect livestock. A female spirit of the juniper tree called Frau Wachholder was called on for retrieving stolen goods.

MAPLE

The maple leaf is the main element of the flag of Canada and is its national emblem. Early North American settlers, who made sugar from the maple, regarded it as a symbol of success and abundance. They would place maple leaves at the foot of the bed to ward off the devil and to encourage the sweetness of conjugal bliss. North American storks (see page 257) use maple branches in their nests, which further associated the tree with love and a new child in the home. In China and Japan, the maple leaf is also an emblem of lovers.

APPLE

In folklore, mythology, and religion, apples appear as a mystical or forbidden fruit. God warned Adam and Eve not to eat of the forbidden fruit (thought to be an apple). They did so and were expelled from the Garden of Eden. Thus the apple became a symbol of sexual seduction. It is also emblematic of discord in the Greek story of the golden apple. In return for a golden apple, Paris of Troy was asked to choose the most beautiful of the goddesses. He selected Aphrodite, enraging the other goddesses, and indirectly causing the Trojan War.

PINE

The ancient Egyptians hollowed out the center of a pine tree and, with the excavated wood, made an image of the tree god Osiris. They then buried the image like a corpse in the hollow of the tree, which was kept for a year and then burned. The pine tree was also associated with the Greek goddess Pitthea and with the wine god Dionysus. Worshippers of Dionysus often carried a cone-tipped wand, because the pine cone was an ancient fertility amulet. For the Romans, the pine tree was worshipped during the spring equinox festival of Cybele and Attis. As an evergreen tree, the pine also symbolized immortality.

Mongolian shamans, or traditional healers, entered pine forests in silence, with reverence for the gods and spirits thought to be living within. In ancient Celtic lands, Druids would light large pine bonfires at the winter solstice to call back the sun. Pine trees were decorated with candles and colorful metallic objects, which gave rise to the tradition of the Christmas tree.

PALM

In ancient Greece and Rome, the palm branch symbolized triumph and victory. The palm was sacred to the god Apollo, who was supposedly born under a palm tree. The Romans gave palm branches as rewards for great athletic achievement or military success. For early Christians, the palm branch symbolized victory over sin and darkness. Today, palm branches are distributed to the faithful on Palm Sunday, the celebration of the triumphal entry of Jesus into Jerusalem.

In Judaism, the palm represents peace and plenty and became a symbol of Judea, where palm trees grow in abundance. The palm may also refer to the Tree of Life in Kabbalah (see page 75). Muhammad is said to have built his home out of palm and the early muezzin may have climbed a palm to call the faithful to prayer. In ancient Assyrian mythology, the palm symbolizes the goddess Ishtar (see page 34). The Mesopotamian goddess Inanna was credited with making dates abundant and humans fertile. The date palm was extremely important to the survival of ancient Near Eastern people because it provided both food and shade.

CROPS AND OTHER PLANTS

Many crops and other useful plants have had symbolic meanings. Because of the importance of agriculture to the survival of ancient civilizations, wheat and corn became enshrined in their mythologies and became emblems of their gods and goddesses. In Asia, the ubiquitous bamboo has many meanings. It is a symbol of Eastern culture and is used on a daily basis for building and other practical uses. It also symbolizes grace and strength; its ability to bend in the wind and not break symbolizes resilience and the gentle Way of the Tao. Bamboo's joined stems also symbolize the Buddhist steps to enlightenment.

CORN

Recent genetic evidence suggests that the domestication of corn, or maize, occurred 9,000 years ago in central Mexico. In North American Navaho culture, the female deity Changing Woman (whose name means "the woman who is transformed time and time again") grows old and becomes young again with the change of the seasons. She also symbolizes the earth and vegetation. For the Navaho, Changing Woman represented corn, reproduction, and the fertility of motherhood.

The Maya and other Mesoamericans (see page 59) considered corn a gift from the gods and cultivating it was a sacred activity. They chose jade (see page 323), a rare and precious stone, to symbolize corn. According to the sacred book of the Maya, the Popol Vuh, man was created from corn. The discovery of the Maize Mountain, where the corn seeds were hidden, is one of the most popular Mayan tales. In another tale, maize or corn is personified as a woman who is a captured bride. The Huichol people of central Mexico still "feed" their newly planted corn with blood from a sacred deer.

WHEAT

The oldest surviving example of wheat found to date is from Çatalhöyük, a Neolithic settlement in southern Anatolia, where the wheat that was discovered was 8,500 years old. To early agricultural peoples, wheat sheaves became symbols of a successful harvest, associated with all that is truly nourishing and life-affirming. Wheat was important to the ancient Chinese, who prayed to the god Hu-tsi, the god of harvests, for a good crop.

In one of the ceremonies of the Eleusinian Mysteries in ancient Greece, a grain of wheat was contemplated in silence. Those taking part in the ritual meditated on the cycles of the seasons and on the miracle of the death of the single seed grain and its subsequent resurrection into a multitude of grains. In this way the participants honored the goddess Demeter, the fertility goddess who ensured the success of the harvest. In Christianity, St. John uses the grain of wheat—which falls on the ground and dies, in order to bring forth much fruit—as a symbol of the resurrection of Christ. In many civilizations, wheat symbolizes the gift of life.

IVY

The clinging aspect of ivy symbolizes true love and faithfulness in marriage and friendship. In Christianity, ivy signifies resurrection and eternal life, as do other evergreens. For medieval Christians, who observed that ivy grew on dead trees, it symbolized the immortal soul that survived the dead body. As it thrives in the shade, ivy is associated with debauchery, carousing, sensuality, and the enjoyment of forbidden pleasures. The satyrs (see page 274) and Dionysus, the god of wine, often wear wreaths of ivy.

CLOVER

The shamrock, a clover with three leaves, is the symbol chosen by St. Patrick of Ireland to represent the Holy Trinity. The Celts revered the clover and had many beliefs based on triads, represented in the triskelion (see page 47), triquetra (see page 83), and triple spiral. The occurrence of threes, as in the clover, was linked to aspects of the Triple Goddess (see page 103) and time's past, present, and future. Clover as a food source for livestock stood for abundance and prosperity and its prolific growth represented sexual reproduction. Clover's sweet smell is said to induce calm and contentment.

BAMBOO

Bamboo is an ancient plant dating back to the time of the dinosaurs. In China, it represents a strong and resilient character. Because it quickly grows high, straight, and strong, the Chinese equate bamboo with straightforward, sincere, and spiritual people and with the Way of the Tao. The linked stems of the bamboo also stand for the Buddhist path to enlightenment. An essential element of formal Chinese and Japanese gardens, it is appreciated for its beauty, the soft sound of its leaves in the breeze, and the delicate shadows that it casts on garden walls. Bamboo groves are thought to induce calm and stimulate creativity. Bamboo symbolizes the virtues of the ideal scholar: purity, longevity, and flexibility. Bamboos provide shade, housing, and many ritual and everyday items, including musical instruments, cooking utensils, furniture, baskets, lampshades, and hats. There is great reverence and respect for bamboo. The mother bamboo plant with her seedlings all around her symbolizes fertility and the happy family. Bamboo has been a symbol of good fortune in Asian cultures for thousands of years.

HERBS AND SPICES

Herbs and spices have stood as symbols from ancient times. The Greeks bestowed wreaths of bay laurel as a symbol of triumph and peace (the term "poet laureate" derives from this practice). In the Middle Ages, herbs not only had symbolic meanings but were also believed to have potent magical powers.

PARSLEY

Parsley was placed on graves to please Persephone, who guided the souls of the dead to the underworld. Homer wrote that warriors fed their horses parsley to help them run faster. The Romans wore parsley sprigs in their togas to protect against evil and placed parsley on plates of food against contamination. Botanist William Turner (1508–1568) wrote that parsley thrown in a pond could cure sick fish.

BASIL

Holy basil, or *tulsi*, is revered in Hinduism and used in the Greek Orthodox Church to prepare holy water. In Europe, basil is placed on the chest of the deceased to ensure a safe journey to heaven. In Africa basil is said to protect against scorpions. In Elizabethan England, guests were given basil to ensure safe passage home. In Italy, a basil plant on a balcony announced that a woman was ready to be courted.

LEMON BALM

Lemon balm is a mint with a lemon scent. For thousands of years herbalists have used it to treat disorders of the nervous system. According to *The London Dispensary* of 1696, lemon balm was given to strengthen the brain, relieve depression, and improve memory. A 17th-century tincture called Carmelite water, made of lemon balm, lemon peel, angelica root, and nutmeg, was used to treat headaches. Today herbalists prescribe lemon balm as a treatment for viral infections such as herpes and cold sores.

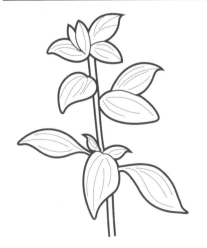

MARJORAM

The Greeks believed that marjoram growing on a grave signaled that the deceased was in a happy place. Both Greeks and Romans crowned young married couples with marjoram. Medicinally, the Greeks used marjoram extensively, both internally for a variety of ailments and externally as a poultice. According to folk medicine, marjoram oil placed in the hollow of an aching tooth relieves pain. Some horse owners use the scent of marjoram oil to calm sexually excited stallions and to sedate horses when transporting them.

MINT

In Greek mythology, Minthe, a naiad, was impressed by Hades' golden chariot. As she was about to be seduced by him, Persephone intervened and metamorphosed her into the sweet-smelling herb of mint. In ancient Greece, mint was used in funerary rites to offset the smell of decay. It was also an ingredient in the fermented barley drink called *kykeon*, a preparatory psychoactive substance for participants in the Eleusinian Mysteries, which offered the hope of a positive afterlife for initiates. In Central and South America, mint is known as *hierbabuena*, or the "good herb."

ROSEMARY

Symbolizing remembrance and fidelity, rosemary was therefore used as decoration at both weddings and funerals. Anne of Cleves, the fourth wife of Henry VIII of England, wore a rosemary wreath at her wedding and rosemary branches gilded and tied with colorful silken ribbons were presented to wedding guests. In old Europe, sprigs of rosemary were dropped on coffins, symbolizing that the deceased would not be forgotten. Ancient Greek students wore rosemary to enhance their memory during examinations.

SAGE

The ancient Greeks and Romans believed sage imparted wisdom and intelligence. Tenth-century Arab physicians associated it with long life. In the 17th century, the English royal family had their servants scatter sage and lavender (see page 298) in order to hide the stench of the "great unwashed." In the Middle Ages, sage was used to treat memory loss, fevers, and intestinal problems. And First Nations peoples in North America use sage tied in bundles for "smudging" or purification; the bundle is lit and passed around a room or space to cleanse and purify the area.

THYME

The name thyme comes from the Greek *thymos*, meaning "spirit." To the ancient Greeks, thyme restored spirit or vigor. It symbolized graceful elegance, and smelling of thyme was an admirable quality. Roman soldiers bathed in thyme to gain strength and courage for battle. During the Middle Ages, knights wore a sprig of thyme embroidered on their scarves as a sign of their bravery. For ancient Greeks, thyme symbolized sweetness. And the honey produced by bees that live near fields of thyme is still considered exceptionally sweet.

GARLIC

Garlic was placed by ancient Greeks on piles of stones at crossroads, as a food offering for the goddess of crossroads, Hecate. A Christian legend relates that when Satan stepped out from the Garden of Eden after the fall of man, garlic sprang up from the spot where he placed his left foot, and an onion from where he placed his right. In many cultures throughout time, garlic was praised for its medicinal uses—especially in warding off infections and in strengthening immunity. It is also thought to be a vampire-repellent.

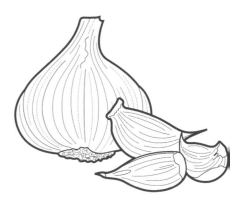

LAVENDER

In Roman times, lavender was used to scent bath water and its name comes from the Latin *lavare*, "to wash." The Romans recognized lavender for its healing and antiseptic qualities and for its usefulness in deterring insects. Dioscorides (c. 40–c. 90 CE), a Greek military physician under the Roman emperor Nero, noted that lavender could be used to clean wounds and burns, or to treat skin ailments. Roman soldiers took lavender with them on campaigns to dress war wounds. Lavender was also strewn on the floor to sweeten the air and fumigate sick rooms.

MISTLETOE

In European folklore, mistletoe is a symbol of fertility and a protection against poison. As an evergreen that produces bright-red berries in midwinter, it symbolized renewal and regeneration. Druids considered mistletoe an aphrodisiac and gathered it from oak trees at the winter solstice. The custom of kissing under mistletoe at Christmas is a survival of this tradition. In the Middle Ages and later on, branches of mistletoe were hung from ceilings to ward off evil spirits and over doors to prevent the entrance of witches.

SAFFRON

Saffron is a spice derived from the stigmas (female parts) of saffron crocus flowers. In the ancient world, the saffron dye and spice obtained from the three female stigmas of each bloom had a value greater than jewels or precious metals, and saffron remains a costly spice today. Saffron was used to dye the garments of women of high status, such as priestesses, in shades from pale yellow to a deep orange-red. In the East, to the present day, saffron-colored robes are associated with Buddhist and Hindu divinities, as well as with monks and nuns.

FLOWERS

The symbolic meaning of flowers has varied widely from culture to culture. For example, in 19th-century England the language of flowers was cultivated as a social art. Directories were written to define the meaning of every flower, such as sympathy, love, or rejection, and gift bouquets called "tussie-mussies" were given to convey a secret message to the recipient. In every culture, however, flowers communicate the poignant beauty and brevity of life.

LILY

In present times, lilies are often associated with whiteness and purity of heart, innocence and virginity, and even with heaven and death. Bouquets of white lilies are popular in Christian homes during the Easter holiday as they symbolize Christ's resurrection. The Easter lily, in the shape of a trumpet, heralds the coming of spring.

In other Christian tradition, the Madonna lily is considered the special flower of the Holy Virgin Mary.

In Roman mythology, the lily is linked to Venus and the satyrs (see page 274), its phallic pistil representing procreation. Poets, such as the French poet Stéphane Mallarmé (1842–1898), suggest that lilies are lunar and female, and so they are associated with love and sensuality. In medieval times, lilies symbolized feminine sexuality, but afterward the sensuous lily was perceived through the eyes of repression to become glorious and pure.

In China, the day lily is the emblem of motherhood. The lily also symbolizes harmony and is often given as a wedding gift. Spaniards believed that eating a lily's petals would restore their humanity after they had behaved in a beastly fashion.

ROSE

For the ancient Greeks and Romans, the rose symbolized love and beauty and the goddesses of love—Aphrodite and Venus. Aphrodite gave a rose to her son Eros, the god of love, who in turn gave it to Harpocrates, the god of silence, to ensure that his mother's indiscretions remained secret. In ancient Rome, a rose would be placed on the door of a room where confidential matters were discussed. From this practice derives the phrase *sub rosa*, or "under the rose," which means "to keep a secret." In the Christian tradition, the phrase *sub rosa* was associated with confession and roses were often carved on confessionals, indicating that the priest would maintain secrecy.

The red rose eventually became a symbol of the blood of Christian martyrs and of the Virgin Mary (see also page 94). It was also used as a badge by marchers in the May 1968 student protests in Paris and has been adopted as a symbol by various European Socialist parties. The rose is also the national flower of both England and the United States.

DAFFODIL

Today, the daffodil symbolizes spring, rebirth, and new beginnings. However, the ancient Greeks associated it with death. Daffodils grew in the meadows where the god Hades captured the goddess Persephone and took her to the underworld. The alternate name for daffodil is narcissus and it is associated with the handsome Greek youth, Narcissus. While walking by a river, he stopped to drink and, taken by his own reflection, he leaned over the water too far, like a drooping daffodil, and drowned.

TULIP

Tulips are associated with Holland, but the flower and its name originated in the Ottoman Empire. They were called *tulipan* after the word *tulbend*, meaning "turban." In early 17th-century Europe, "tulipmania" took hold and the wealthy traded bulbs like stocks and shares. The tulip as a status symbol was then used extensively as a decorative motif in wealthy homes. In early 20th-century America, the tulip became a symbol of hope and post-war wealth, and this prosperous-looking flower is often chosen as a logo for financial institutions.

HYACINTH

In Greek mythology, the hyacinth is associated with the prince Hyacinthus, a beautiful youth loved by the god Apollo. Throwing the discus very hard to impress Hyacinthus, Apollo accidentally killed him and the hyacinth sprang from the blood of the dying prince. Another version states that the wind god Zephyrus was jealous of Hyacinthus' love for Apollo and blew Apollo's discus off course, killing Hyacinthus. When he died, Apollo refused to let Hades claim the boy. Instead, he created the hyacinth flower from the prince's spilled blood.

DAISY

The daisy gets its name from the Anglo-Saxon term *daes eage*, or "day's eye," referring to the way in which it opens and closes with the sun. Chaucer called it "eye of the day." The daisy is associated with childhood innocence, simplicity, and modesty. Girls still pluck a daisy's petals one by one, repeating "He loves me, he loves me not." When farmers in old England dreamed of daisies in the springtime, they considered it a lucky omen; dreams of daisies in the autumn or winter signaled bad luck.

CARNATION

A red carnation symbolizes passionate and pure love; a pink carnation symbolizes marriage. During the Renaissance, a carnation represented the vow of fidelity and the groom presented the bride with one at the wedding. Rembrandt's portrait *Woman with a Pink* shows a woman holding a pink carnation, symbolizing her marriage to the man in another of his portraits, *Man with a Magnifying Glass*. In Christian legend, Mary wept as she watched Jesus carrying the cross and where her tears fell carnations grew; carnations often appear in paintings of her.

CHRYSANTHEMUM

In ancient China, the chrysanthemum symbolized cheerfulness and rest after the final harvest. Around the 8th century CE the chrysanthemum appeared in Japan and so impressed the emperor that he made it his official crest and seal. For the Japanese, the chrysanthemum is a symbol of the sun and the orderly unfolding of its petals is a symbol of perfection. Japan even has a national chrysanthemum day known as the Festival of Happiness. In Italy, the chrysanthemum is associated with the dead and with funerals.

IRIS

Iris, which in Greek means "rainbow," gets its name from the Greek goddess of the rainbow, who carried messages from the gods on Mount Olympus to humans. The iris symbolizes royalty and divine protection. The fleur-de-lis, a stylized iris motif, has stood for France and its royalty since the 12th century. During the reign of Louis IX in the 13th century, the three petals of the fleur-de-lis came to represent faith, wisdom, and valor, and were said to be a symbol of divine favor bestowed on France. The iris functions as both the national flower and the emblem of France.

MARIGOLD

Marigolds, one of the most widely cultivated flowers in India, are harvested by hand so as not to damage the delicate blooms. Loose marigold blooms or garlands are sold in markets for religious decoration and for offerings. Bright-yellow and orange marigold garlands decorate statues and temples and are offered at funerals, weddings, and other ceremonies. Boiling the flowers produces a yellow dye. Old English herbals recommend marigold flowers as a remedy for bee stings, while Mexicans decorate graves with marigolds on the Day of the Dead.

LILAC

Lilacs belong to the genus *Syringa*, the name deriving from the Greek word *syrinx*, meaning a pipe or flute. In Greek mythology, the nymph Syrinx turned herself into a reed to hide from Pan. Pan used the reed to make the first flute. Purple lilacs symbolize first love, while white lilacs embody youthful innocence.

In contemporary Greece, Lebanon, and Cyprus, the lilac is strongly associated with Easter because it first blooms around that time. Consequently the lilac there is called *paschalia*. Lilacs are also associated with grief and mourning. In the late 19th century, in Europe and North America, black was worn to symbolize a recent death, but after a year of mourning a widow could change the color of her clothing to lilac. "When Lilacs Last in the Door-yard Bloom'd" is an elegy on the death of President Abraham Lincoln (1809–1865), written by the American poet Walt Whitman (1819–1892). Whitman expresses his grief at the loss of Lincoln and grapples with death itself. Like other shades of purple (see page 390), lilac also symbolizes spirituality.

LOTUS

The lotus is one of the most illustrative symbols of Buddhism (see page 134). It has its roots in the mud, its stem grows up through the water, and the heavily scented flower emerges on top of the water in full sunlight. The lotus, then, becomes the metaphor for the journey of the soul from the primeval mud of suffering, through the waters of spiritual practice, into the bright sunshine of enlightenment. In Buddhism, the human heart is referred to as an unopened lotus, the pristine Buddha nature within waiting to bloom. In many representations of the Buddha, he sits on a lotus throne, and numerous Buddhist deities are depicted either sitting on or holding a lotus flower.

The white lotus is associated with the White Tara and proclaims her perfect nature. The pink lotus is linked with the Buddha himself. The red lotus is the lotus of love and compassion and is the flower of Avalokiteshvara, the bodhisattva of compassion. The blue lotus is a symbol of wisdom and an emblem of Manjushri, the bodhisattva of wisdom.

POPPY

In Greek and Roman mythology, poppies were a symbol of both sleep and death. The opium extracted from poppies caused sleep and their blood-red color stood for death as well as for resurrection from the dead. In these ancient cultures, poppies were used as offerings for the deceased. Today, poppies are carved as decorations on tombstones to symbolize eternal sleep. In Europe, the corn poppy became a symbol of the fallen soldier in the First World War, because it was the only plant that continued to grow in the war-torn fields. On Remembrance Day in Commonwealth countries, and also on Memorial Day in the United States, plastic and paper poppies are worn to remember the veterans of war.

In the East, the drug opium is extracted from the poppy. The drug was known in ancient Greece and Rome and was originally used only as a sedative and for pain relief. Later, in other cultures, it was used as a recreational drug for pleasure. Opium is also one of the most valuable medicinal drugs and morphine and codeine (the two principal alkaloids of the poppy) are extensively used.

ORCHID

The orchid's name derives from the Greek word *orchis*, meaning "testicle." In ancient times, Greek women tried to influence the sex of their unborn children with orchid roots. The father would eat large new tubers if a male child was wanted and the mother would eat small tubers if she wanted a female child. The *Paphiopedilum* orchid was named for Paphos, the temple of the love goddess Aphrodite, located on the island of Cyprus. Perhaps the most famous orchid is the vanilla orchid, the source of vanilla flavoring.

THISTLE

The Scottish thistle, a thorny yet beautiful flowering plant, is an ancient Celtic symbol of pain and suffering, as well as of noble character and birth. King James V of Scotland (1512–1542) instituted the Order of the Thistle, one of the most ancient British Orders, in 1540. The motto of the Order was *Nemo me impune lacessit* ("No one provokes me with impunity"). In 1262, when the Danes tried to attack Scotland at night, one of the barefoot soldiers yelled in pain as he stepped on a prickly thistle, thus alerting the Scots to the Danish invasion.

MINERALS, CRYSTALS, AND GEMSTONES

From earliest times, humans have been drawn to minerals, crystals, and gemstones for their color, beauty, and energetic qualities. Stones were used for practical purposes, such as for tools and weapons, but also for magic and healing. Gemstones were portals for psychic powers, their energies conduits for divine guidance and spiritual advancement. Human interest in gemstones has continued unabated since the dawn of humankind, as demonstrated by their ongoing use for adornment, energetic healing, and spiritual development in every culture on the planet.

MINERALS

Throughout ancient times, minerals or metals were linked to fire and melting. For alchemists, the extraction of metals from ore and their refinement were associated with spiritual testing and purification. Minerals, which are found underground, symbolize human sensuality in need of transformation. In spiritual initiations, initiates are often asked to remove metal jewelry to symbolize purification and the renunciation of worldly possessions. While precious metals, such as gold, silver, and platinum, have been highly prized by all cultures since antiquity, iron is the most abundant metal, accounting for 95 percent of metal production worldwide. Tin has also been crucial in mankind's development: combined with copper it made possible the making of bronze.

PLATINUM

In the periodic table, platinum is given the letters Pt. It is an extremely rare metal—30 times rarer than gold and twice the price. When pure, platinum is a beautiful silvery-white and corrosion-resistant. It symbolizes endurance, determination, grit, and seeing work through to completion. In the 18th century, King Louis XV of France declared it the most appropriate metal for a king. The first British crown to be made of platinum was for Queen Elizabeth, the Queen Mother, which was created for her coronation as consort of King George VI in 1937. In popular culture, platinum is associated with exclusivity and wealth.

GOLD

The element gold is represented by the letters Au. In most cultures, gold is regarded as the most precious and perfect of all metals. As it never tarnishes and flashes brightly in the sun, in India gold is called "mineral light." Throughout most of the world it is revered for its rarity, beauty, and its fiery, solar, masculine nature. Gold is often associated with royalty and the divine. The ancient Egyptians believed that the flesh of the gods was made of gold. Images of the Buddha are often gilded, a sign of enlightenment and perfection. Medieval kings were inaugurated with a golden crown that symbolized their divinely or heavenly inspired authority (see page 162). Wedding rings are traditionally gold, representing a lasting relationship untarnished by the passage of time.

Gold has been associated with sin— as in the story of the golden calf in the Book of Exodus, a symbol of idolatry and a turning away from God. Bags of gold coins are a symbol of extreme wealth when juxtaposed with the poverty of the masses and extraordinary achievements are often rewarded with gold medals, such as those of the Olympic Games. (See also page 201.)

IRON

Iron is represented by the letters Fe. The most abundant element on earth, it makes up about 5 percent of the earth's crust and 35 percent of its core. It symbolizes brute-like strength, as well as durability, hardness, and inflexibility. For the Greek poet Hesiod, writing c. 700 BCE, iron stood for materialism, force, and the primitive and unconscious mind. According to Plato (c. 428–348 BCE), iron came from the underworld and needed to be contained and kept separate from everyday life. The Druids avoided the use of iron implements in their sacred ceremonies.

In some cultures iron is considered a dark, base metal, in comparison to the bright metals of copper and bronze that are thought to be noble. For the Dogon people of Mali, iron represents the Lord of Darkness, the evil demiurge Yurugu, the jackal god who rules divination, barrenness, drought, and death. However, the all-powerful Lord of Heaven, the demiurge Nommo, created the blacksmith who could make Yurugu's iron his servant, by fashioning it into farm tools and hunting weapons. In Mali, the blacksmith is often also the village fortune-teller.

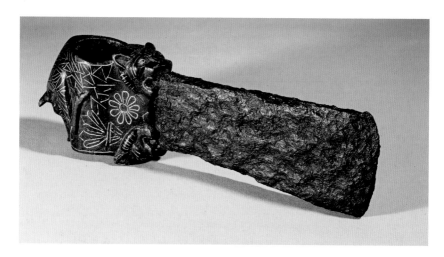

SILVER

Silver is represented by the letters Ag. It relates to the moon, water, and the feminine principle. White and shining, silver stands for purity, a clear conscience, pure intent, and good-heartedness. Silver

represents divine wisdom in Christianity. According to ancient Egyptian myths, the flesh of the gods was gold, but their bones were made of silver. In Russian folklore, the tarnishing of silver items such as forks or snuffboxes was a sign that the hero in the tale was in danger. In other European folklore, silver is an antidote to and repellent of vampires. Mirrors were originally made from polished silver and vampires—not having a soul—could not see themselves in them. Only a bullet made of silver could kill a werewolf. The term "silver bullet" indicates a specific remedy for a problem. (See also page 201.)

TIN

Tin is represented by the letters Sn. The highly crystalline structure of this malleable, silvery-white metal causes a characteristic crackling sound when bent. Used to harden copper to make bronze implements from as early as 3,500 BCE, tin suggests the idea of strength through joining together with others. Tin is also associated with the planet Jupiter (see page 213) and the zodiacal sign Sagittarius (see page 206). Because of its relationship with Jupiter, this metal symbolizes both breathing and the breath of life.

CRYSTALS AND GEMSTONES

In Egypt, gemstones were used to protect the dead in the afterlife; pieces of unworn jewelry made of gold, turquoise, obsidian, rock crystal, and other stones were found in the tomb of Tutankhamun. The Egyptians also wore jewelry in everyday life, with some rings functioning as cylinder seals, and by the Roman era it was common to give rings for birthdays. The Greeks, Arabs, and others wrote about the practical, medicinal, and spiritual qualities of stones in texts called lapidaries. The oldest Western lapidary was written by the Greek Theophrastus in around 300 BCE. During the medieval era there was great interest in the use of stones for healing and wealthy Europeans wore amulets made of crystals and stones for various ailments.

RUBY

Ruby is the red variety of the mineral corundum and is associated with unbridled love, passion, and power. In Christian lore, it was considered an emblem of good fortune, banishing sorrow and warding off negative thoughts. As a healing stone, the ruby balances the heart and circulatory system, combats exhaustion, and imparts vigor. It detoxifies the blood and lymph and treats infections. Psychologically, the ruby brings about a positive and courageous state of mind and promotes enthusiasm for life.

CORAL

Corals are marine organisms that secrete calcium carbonate to form a hard skeleton. The skeleton grows into tree shapes, forming the coral reefs of the world. Since ancient times, coral has been used for jewelry-making and as a protective amulet. The ancient Romans put red coral necklaces and bracelets on their children to protect them from danger. Today, in many cultures, red corals are still worn as a talisman to protect the wearer against the evil eye. In China, coral is a symbol of longevity and in India it is said to prevent hemorrhages. In Tibet, red coral is said to encourage passion and to stimulate and strengthen the female reproductive organs. Red coral is one of the five sacred stones of the Tibetan Buddhists and symbolizes the energy of the life force. The Tibetans and Nepalese think of coral as a good investment and they believe that the person who wears coral will be successful in life.

CINNABAR

Cinnabar was mined during the Roman Empire both as a pigment and for its mercury content. It has been the main source of mercury throughout the centuries. The red stone was used as decoration in royal Mayan burial chambers. The Byzantine emperor signed his name with ink made red by the addition of cinnabar. On an energy level, cinnabar is said to attract abundance and prosperity without the use of aggression. It also helps with community organization, business, and finance.

CARNELIAN

Some of the oldest examples of human jewelry contain carnelian—ancient Egyptians wore carnelian jewelry and amulets to ensure their soul's passage into the next world. Muslims engrave the name of Allah on carnelian stones to boost courage. In Hebrew legend, carnelian appears as a stone in Aaron's breastplate. Psychologically, carnelian is said to help with the acceptance of death as part of life. As a healing stone, it helps with sexual frigidity and impotence and lower back pain, and positively influences the female reproductive organs.

AMBER

Amber is not a crystal or gemstone, but rather a 30–90-million-year-old fossilized tree resin. It is yellow-orange in color and sometimes contains insects or small vertebrates. Appreciated since ancient times for its color and beauty, amber is used for jewelry and other decorative objects. The most highly prized amber is transparent. As an amulet, it is considered a powerful healer and cleanser of the body and the environment. It is said to absorb negative forces and stimulate positive ones that bring healing and balance to life.

TIGER'S EYE

Tiger's eye is a gemstone that is usually yellow to red-brown, with undulating, contrasting bands of color. In many cultures, tiger's eye has functioned as a protective stone against curses and ill wishes. Containing energies of both the earth and the sun, tiger's eye possesses a high, yet grounded vibration. It helps distinguish between flights of fantasy and what is really needed in life. As a healing stone, tiger's eye aids problems with the eyes and reproductive organs. It can balance masculine and feminine energies and the emotions.

GARNET

Garnets have a high refractive value and it is said that travelers used to carry garnets with them to light up the night and protect them from disaster. Noah is supposed to have used a garnet lantern to help him steer his ark through the darkness. Garnets are found in jewelry from early Egyptian, Greek, and Roman times. Today, the garnet is thought to be a powerfully energizing and regenerating stone. It helps bring clarity to self-perception and the perceptions of others, and stimulates sluggish metabolism.

JASPER

Jasper is an opaque, impure variety of silica, often red, yellow, or green in color. The ancient Babylonians, Greco-Romans, and medieval Europeans associated jasper with women's diseases and childbirth. This was perhaps because jasper would shatter into several stones. Also, in all these cultures metals were considered to be alive, having grown in the womb of the earth. Red jasper is said to help in owning one's personal power, calming aggressive energy and removing feelings of victimization. Yellow jasper is believed to balance the female hormones. Green jasper helps with recovery from burnout.

CITRINE

Not to be confused with commercial citrine, which is artificially heated amethyst or smoky quartz, naturally occurring citrine is a yellow to brown quartz that is highly prized, especially the darker colors. Crystal healers believe citrine is one of the very rare stones that do not accumulate negative energy, but rather dissipate and transmute it. Unlike other crystals, it never needs cleansing. It is associated with wealth accumulation, mental focus and stamina, and with the navel and solar plexus chakras (energy centers).

TOPAZ

Topaz is a silicate gemstone most commonly found in yellow tones. Known for at least 2,000 years, it is a symbol of beauty and splendor. The Romans dedicated the topaz to Jupiter. Throughout history it has been known as a bringer of joy, generosity, abundance, and good health. A mellow stone, topaz is said to relieve tension and promote relaxation. It soothes, heals, and renews after prolonged periods of stress. Topaz can support visualization and manifestation, and the successful achievement of earthly goals.

EMERALD

The Incas and Aztecs of South America regarded the emerald as a holy gemstone. The green of the emerald is the color of life, springtime, beauty, and enduring love. In ancient Rome, green was the color of Venus, the goddess of beauty, and love. Alchemists associate the emerald with the god Mercury, the conductor of the souls of the dead. In medieval legends, the emerald was considered a mysterious stone that held tremendous beneficent powers as a talisman. Today, it is a stone symbolizing inspiration and patience.

BLOODSTONE

Bloodstone is green jasper dotted with bright-red spots of iron oxide. Medieval Christians carved scenes of the lives of the martyrs in bloodstone, which they called the "martyrs' stone." According to Christian legend, the bloodstone was first formed when drops of Christ's blood fell and stained the jasper stones at the foot of the cross. In ancient times it was used as an oracle stone, providing guidance to those who could hear its messages. It is said to calm the heart and reduce irritability and aggressiveness. Bloodstone also heightens intuition and creativity.

JADE

The term "jade" is applied to two different rocks that are made up of different silicate minerals: nephrite jade and jadeite. They are both beautifully colored, hard, and tough stones, and can be delicately carved. Of the two, jadeite is more rare. Jade is a yang (see page 146), or masculine, stone with solar and royal associations. In Chinese legend, it was formed in the womb of the earth by lightening. Its beauty makes it a symbol of perfection. Jade also represents righteousness and the moral virtues of charity, prudence, justice, grace, harmony, and sincerity.

The Maya and other Mesoamerican cultures (see page 62) esteemed jadeite not only for its preciousness and beauty but also as stone of great symbolic importance. For them it symbolized royalty, as well as the material embodiment of wind and the vitalizing breath-soul. Jade was an important component of the funerary rites of the Maya and of their ritual conjuring of gods and ancestors.

MOLDAVITE

Moldavite is a green tektite crystal formed by a giant meteorite impact that occurred about 15 million years ago and was found in the Moldau area of the Czech Republic. As such, it is considered a fusion of earth and extraterrestrial energies. Since the Stone Age, moldavite has been used as a talisman for good fortune and fertility. In modern times, gemstone therapists believe that it can put one in touch with one's higher self and even with extraterrestrials. It is said to relieve money worries and concerns about the future.

MALACHITE

Malachite is a beautiful green gemstone with irregular black banding. In ancient Greece, protective amulets made of malachite were attached to infants' cradles. In the Middle Ages, malachite was worn to protect from black magic and sorcery and to detect impending danger. As a healing stone, malachite is said to regenerate the cells of the body and relieve insomnia. Gazing at malachite is believed to relax the nerves and calm angry emotions. Malachite is said to bring peace and harmony into the household.

SAPPHIRE

In earlier times, some cultures believed that the firmament was an enormous blue sapphire in which the earth was embedded. The sapphire appears in every shade of blue and is associated with sympathy, harmony, friendship, and loyalty—everything that is constant and reliable. In Christianity, the sapphire is a symbol of purity and the Kingdom of God. In the East, it is regarded as a charm against the evil eye. The sapphire releases frustration and promotes tranquillity. Placed on the throat, it is said to facilitate self-expression and honesty.

LAPIS LAZULI

Lapis lazuli is a semi-precious stone prized since antiquity for its intense blue color. In the Egyptian Book of the Dead, lapis lazuli, made in the shape of an eye set in gold, was considered one of the most powerful amulets. The Tibetans valued lapis above all minerals and stones, even ahead of gold, and both men and women wore it on their heads. Lapis lazuli is said to open the "third eye" and bring enlightenment. This stone can quickly relieve stress and bring a sense of deep calm and peace.

TURQUOISE

Turquoise is an opaque blue-green mineral esteemed for thousands of years as a sacred stone and talisman. The burial mask of Tutankhamun was liberally inlaid with turquoise. In ancient Persia, turquoise was worn as an amulet for protection against untimely death. If the stone changed color, it was thought to warn against danger or infidelity. Turquoise was worn to ensure prosperity. Placed on a horse's bridle, it was thought to prevent accidents and falls. As a healing stone, turquoise supports the assimilation of nutrients.

AMETHYST

Amethyst is a violet-colored quartz used as semi-precious stone in jewelry-making. The name comes from the ancient Greek word *amethus*, meaning "sober," reflecting the belief that wearing amethyst jewelry, or drinking from vessels made of amethyst, protected the wearer from drunkenness. Orthodox Christian bishops were said to wear amethyst to guard against spiritual or worldly intoxication. As a healing stone, amethyst helps overcome addictions of all kinds. It is said to be beneficial for focusing the mind and to be helpful with decision-making.

OBSIDIAN

Obsidian is a very hard, dark-green to black volcanic rock that is found in desert regions. It is formed when lava cools quickly. Ancient Egyptian sculptors used obsidian to extraordinary effect in its polished form. Among Central American tribes, obsidian was thought to protect against black magic and evil spirits. In contemporary times, it is considered to have truth-telling powers and is helpful in exposing flaws and weaknesses. Psychologically, it helps to integrate the shadow into one's personality.

CHALCEDONY

Chalcedony is a form of silica originally found in the Mediterranean and Asia Minor. It comes in a wide range of colors. On Minoan Crete at the Palace of Knossos, examples of carved chalcedony date to circa 1800 BCE. Because hot wax would not stick to it, it was often used to make official seals. As a healing stone, chalcedony is considered a powerful cleanser of open sores. It helps to increase lactation for nursing mothers and foster the maternal instinct. Psychologically, chalcedony is a nurturing stone that helps promote harmony among family members.

DIAMOND

The diamond is the hardest-known naturally occurring mineral. The name derives from the ancient Greek *adamas*, meaning "invincible." The diamond's hardness and ability to cut are important to Tibetan Buddhists. These attributes are given to the *vajra*, or "diamond thunderbolt," the symbol of immutable and all-conquering spiritual enlightenment. The diamond represents purity and the bonds of relationship, as in the form of a wedding ring. During the Renaissance, it represented equanimity, courage, freedom from fear, integrity, and faith. The bright light of the diamond exposes anything negative in need of transformation.

ONYX

A form of quartz, onyx appears in many colors, but pure black is its most famous form. In European folklore, onyx is used to initiate psychic attacks, especially those of a sexual nature. It is said to be dangerous for pregnant women, causing stillbirths, but in India the opposite is true and onyx protects against the evil eye and eases childbirth. Today, onyx is said to help in difficult circumstances. As it retains memories belonging to the wearer, it is useful for healing old traumas.

QUARTZ

Quartz symbolizes balance and perfection. Dr. John Dee (1527–1608), the famous spiritualist at the court of Queen Elizabeth I, possessed a crystal ball made of smoky quartz. As a healing stone, quartz is considered a master healer, perhaps the most powerful stone on the planet. Quartz generates strong vibrations that cleanse the organs and balance the subtle bodies. When held in the hand, quartz doubles a person's magnetic field. This stone also absorbs negative energy and helps the balanced expression of emotion, thought, and desire. Quartz is said to enhance psychic abilities and the immune system.

MOONSTONE

Moonstone is a soft, milky-white stone resembling the color of the moon. It is a gemstone that belongs to the feldspar family of stone, which accounts for more than half the earth's crust. The moonstone, a sacred stone in India, was placed in the mouth during a full moon in order to correctly predict the future. It has been claimed that moonstone can lead to psychic immortality because it strengthens the spirit so that it can exist outside the body. Legend says that the moonstone arouses tender passion in lovers.

PEARL

Pearls are formed when a foreign particle penetrates the soft tissue of a living mollusk and concentric layers of calcium carbonate form around it, creating the pearl. Perfectly round pearls with a deep luster are the most valuable. Pearls are lunar, feminine, and representative of the Great Mother. They symbolize purity, virginity, and perfection. The "flaming pearl," signifying spiritual consciousness and enlightenment, appears as the third eye of both Shiva (see page 116) and the Buddha. A treasure difficult to attain, such as wisdom, is a "pearl of great price." (See also page 43.)

OPAL

Most opal is more than 60 million years old and dates back to the times when dinosaurs roamed the earth. The most striking quality of opal is its ability to refract and reflect light, giving it its unique visual appeal. A beautiful opal called the Orphanus graced the crown of the Holy Roman Emperor and opals also appear in the Crown Jewels of France. Emotionally, opals symbolize love, passion, desire, and the erotic, and they are known to release inhibitions. When one is very ill, opal encourages the will to live.

TOURMALINE

Tourmaline gemstones are available in a broad range of colors. According to Egyptian legend, the tourmaline passed over a rainbow on its journey up from the center of the earth. Tourmaline can become electrically charged when it is heated and then allowed to cool, having a positive charge at one end and a negative charge at the other. Tourmaline can be used for crystal-gazing to obtain spiritual visions. This stone is also useful for aligning the chakras (energy centers) and balancing the meridians (energy paths) in the body.

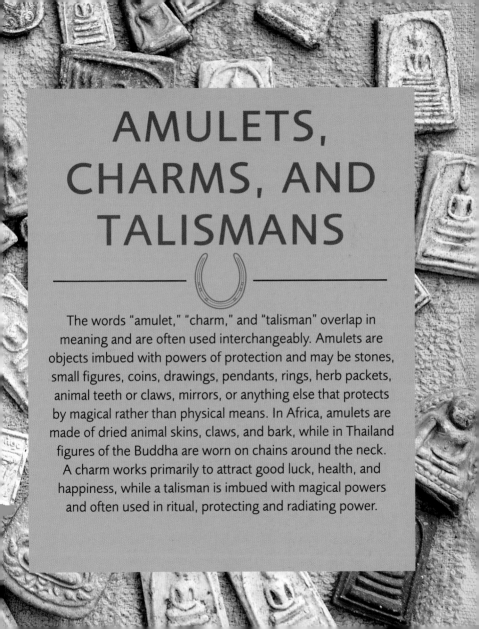

AMULETS, CHARMS, AND TALISMANS

The words "amulet," "charm," and "talisman" overlap in meaning and are often used interchangeably. Amulets are objects imbued with powers of protection and may be stones, small figures, coins, drawings, pendants, rings, herb packets, animal teeth or claws, mirrors, or anything else that protects by magical rather than physical means. In Africa, amulets are made of dried animal skins, claws, and bark, while in Thailand figures of the Buddha are worn on chains around the neck. A charm works primarily to attract good luck, health, and happiness, while a talisman is imbued with magical powers and often used in ritual, protecting and radiating power.

AMULETS OF PROTECTION

People wear amulets to protect them from other people, bullets, witches, evil spirits, the devil, vampires, and negative energy of all kinds—especially that of the "evil eye," or the envious gaze of others. Protection is desired for babies and children as well as adults, bicycles, cars, animals, and even farm implements. Amulets used for protection are found everywhere in the world and often mix standard religious symbols with folk tales and mythology. In the Islamic world, the hand of Fatima and blue beads are worn to ward off the evil eye. In the West, the crucifix is worn as a declaration of religious faith as well as for protection. The American astronaut Edward White (1930–1967) went into space with a St. Christopher's medal in his pocket.

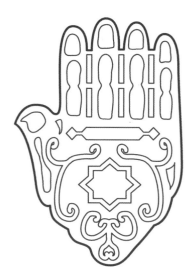

MIDDLE EASTERN HAMSA HAND/HAND OF FATIMA

Many cultures believe that good fortune may attract the jealousy of others who, as a result, will bestow a curse through a malevolent gaze called the "evil eye." The hamsa hand is a symbol used in amulets, charms, and jewelry to protect against the evil eye. Another name for this amulet is the hand of Fatima (see page 107), in reference to Fatima Zahra, the daughter of Muhammad. Hamsas are popular in Israel simply as a symbol of good luck. Many Jewish hamsas are decorated with fish or Hebrew prayers.

MIDDLE EASTERN BLUE EYE

A blue eye, also called a *nazar* or evil-eye stone, is an amulet dating back to ancient mythology that is said to protect against the evil eye. It consists of concentric circles, with dark blue on the outside, then light blue or yellow, and finally white with a small dark-blue center resembling a blue eye. It is thought that the blue-eye amulet originally derives from the Egyptian Eye of Horus amulet, which is also used for warding off the evil eye (see page 25). The use of blue-eye amulets is widespread throughout the eastern Mediterranean and the Middle East.

MEXICAN OJO DE DIOS

The Mexican *ojo de Dios*, or eye of God, is a magical object that symbolizes the power of being able to see what is unknowable. The prayer expressed by the maker is that the all-seeing eye of God will rest upon the supplicant. The *ojo de Dios* is a weaving usually made of colored yarn wound around two crossed sticks at right angles. The resultant lozenge shapes create four points representing the elements of earth, fire, air, and water. The *ojo de Dios* is thought to have originated with the Huichol people of Mexico.

ITALIAN HORN

The Italian horn, or *corno*, is an ancient amulet once sacred to the pre-Christian European moon goddess, whose consort was sometimes called the Horned God. A *corno* is a long, gently twisted, horn-shaped amulet worn to protect against the evil eye. It is often carved out of red coral or made of gold or silver. Today the *corno* is found in Italy and in the U.S. among descendants of Italian immigrants, and is worn by boys and men to protect their genitalia from the evil eye.

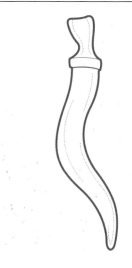

TIBETAN NAMKHA

In the Vajrayana Buddhist tradition, the *namkha* is constructed as the temporary dwelling for a deity during ritual practice. It is made from threads woven around sticks, traditionally using colored thread that is symbolic of the elements: blue stands for space, green stands for air, red stands for fire, white stands for water, and yellow stands for earth. Each deity determines the sequence and shape of the *namkha*. Tibetan *namkhas* may also be used to capture malevolent spirits or thoughts. The threads symbolize that each point in time and space is the warp and weft of the loom of emptiness, the basis of wisdom and enlightenment.

ROMAN CATHOLIC POWERFUL HAND

A famous talisman in London's British Museum is a late-Roman sculpture known as the Hand of Power, or *Mano Panthea*. The descendant of the Hand of Power is the powerful hand, or *mano poderosa*, of Roman Catholicism, which is often depicted on holy cards and votive candles. In the modern Catholic version, the figures on top of the four fingers represent St. Joseph, the Virgin Mary, and her parents, St. Joachim and St. Anne, with the Christ Child on the thumb. The meaning of the hand is the same as in ancient times: magical protection and benediction.

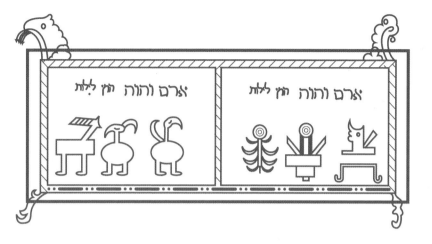

JEWISH LILITH PROTECTION AMULET

In Jewish lore, Lilith was the first wife of Adam, but she refused to be dominated—sexually or otherwise—and abandoned him. She then had erotic encounters with fallen angels and gave birth to an enormous family of demons called the lilim. Adam wanted her back, so God sent three angels, Senoy, Sansenoy, and Semangelof, to threaten her that if she did not return, 100 of her sons would die every day. She refused, but said that she would seek revenge for the deaths of her children, vowing to kill newborn infants and women in childbirth. However, she agreed that she would not harm any infant or mother wearing an amulet with the images or names of the three angels inscribed upon it.

Lilith amulets are made of silver or paper, or are drawn on the wall as a circle of protection, with the names of the three angels written within. Perhaps because of Lilith's highly sexual nature, women also used her amulet to increase their fertility.

PENNSYLVANIAN HEX SIGNS

The practice of painting hex designs on buildings, as a means of protection against witchcraft, negative rune workings, and spells, represents a positive talisman and dates back to the pre-Christian era in Europe. The term "hex" may derive from the German *Hexe*, meaning "witch," or from the Greek prefix *hex-*, meaning "six"—six-sided designs protecting against hexes were common on early Germanic homes and can still be seen above the doors of some buildings. These brightly colored, geometric designs are today best known as an aspect of the Pennsylvanian Dutch folk art of North America, although the hex signs seen on Dutch barns in central and eastern Pennsylvania are not six-sided and are mostly decorative in nature.

TRIPLE STAR

LUCKY STARS

OAK LEAVES
AND ACORNS

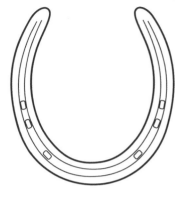

HORSESHOE

The practice of using worn horseshoes as protective talismans originated in Europe, where farmers would nail them above the doors of houses, barns, and stables to ward off evil spirits. The crescent shape of the horseshoe evokes the moon and the Greek and Roman moon goddesses Artemis and Diana. The horseshoe represents the Mother Goddess as protectress, symbolizing the fruitfulness of her sacred vulva and womb, and is also related to other protective doorway goddesses, such as the Irish Sheela-na-Gig (see page 55), the Roman goddess Cardea, and the Blessed Virgin, who is often shown standing on a crescent-shaped moon and placed within a vulva-shaped mandorla (when two circles overlap one another, the space in between forms an almond shape, pointed at both ends, known as the mandorla).

The horseshoe is one of the most common talismans seen in modern North America. If used in its function as a talisman for magical protection, placed over the doorways of barns and stables, the horseshoe is placed with the ends pointing downward. However, today it is usually placed upward, in its function as a container or vessel of good luck. In Mexico, used horseshoes are wrapped in colorful thread and sequins, and are sold with holy cards of San Martin Caballero, the horse-rider.

FOR GOOD LUCK AND PROSPERITY

Good-luck charms come in many different shapes and forms. Examples include a rabbit's foot or a four-leafed clover carried on a key chain to bring good luck. In China, crickets in cages are thought to bring good fortune and coins tossed onto the floor are said to bring money. The Japanese maneki neko, which is also called the lucky or beckoning cat, is said to attract customers to businesses when placed beside a cash register.

TIBETAN PRAYER FLAGS

For centuries Tibetan Buddhists have used prayer flags as talismans for longevity, peace, happiness, and prosperity. As the wind blows the flag, it is said to carry the prayers and mantras of the deities and protectors that are printed on it, in order to spread peace and prosperity to all it touches. There are two types of prayer flag: the long strings of flags that are hoisted horizontally between trees or pillars, with five colored flags repeated in a sequence; and narrow flags that are flown vertically on a pole or can be planted in the ground.

AMERICAN RABBIT'S FOOT

The rabbit's foot is recognized throughout American culture as a good-luck symbol, but its origin is in the southern, African-American folk-magic tradition. Only the left hind foot of the rabbit was considered lucky and it had to be rubbed in order to bring luck. The auspicious rabbit's foot may be an outgrowth of Br'er Rabbit, the protagonist in the *Uncle Remus* novels of Joel Chandler Harris (1848–1908), an amalgamation of Cherokee and African trickster-rabbit myths. Today, the rabbit's foot is less popular because of animal-rights issues.

LATIN AMERICAN LODESTONES

A lodestone is a natural magnet. Because of its inherent drawing power, the ancient Romans valued the lodestone as a powerful amulet for increasing power and prosperity. Lodestones are vital in African-American hoodoo (traditional folk magic) practice, and in Latin American *budu* magic. In Latin America, lodestones are found in packages of amulets for drawing money toward the wearer. The lodestones are sprinkled with magnetic sand or ultra-fine iron shot to enhance their power and may also be rubbed with anointing oil.

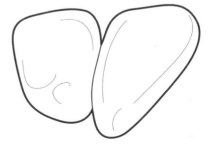

JAPANESE MANEKI NEKO

The maneki neko, which means "beckoning cat," is a common Japanese ceramic figurine believed to bring good luck. The sculpture depicts a white cat beckoning with an upright paw and is usually displayed at the entrance of shops and restaurants. The origin of this charm is as follows: one day a samurai passed a cat that seemed to wave at him. Taking the cat's wave as a sign, he went to it and, in doing so, avoided a trap that had been laid for him just ahead. Ever since then cats have been considered lucky spirits.

CHINESE BA GUA MIRROR

The I Ching is a system of yin and yang (see page 146) which comprises eight trigrams (see page 148), which in turn form 64 hexagrams. In Chinese, *ba* is the number eight and *gua* means "trigram," and so the term *ba gua* signifies the eight trigrams. *Ba gua* mirrors are octagonal *ba guas* with mirrors in the center. They are used to bring harmony and prosperity to a home or office. Ideally, they should be placed near the center of a room or building. They are also frequently hung above the doors of homes and businesses to bring good luck to all who enter.

CHINESE MONEY TOAD

Chan chu is the name of the lucky money toad, a popular symbol for prosperity that is usually seen in Chinese restaurants and shops. It generally has red eyes and flared nostrils and sits on a pile of money, while holding a coin in its mouth. According to Feng Shui lore, it is believed to protect wealth and increase income. Money toads are placed facing the front door, to invite money in, and are turned backward at night to prevent the newly earned money from leaving.

JAPANESE DARUMA DOLL

Daruma dolls are hollow, round Japanese wish-dolls with no arms or legs, said to represent Bodhidharma, the founder and first patriarch of Zen. The rounded, weighted doll is painted red, with a face with a moustache, beard, and blank white circles for eyes. Using black ink, the owner of the doll fills in the right eye while making a wish. Should the wish later come true, the remaining eye is filled in. Until the wish has been granted, the daruma doll is kept in a high place, often near the Buddhist home altar.

Daruma dolls are usually purchased in or near Buddhist temples. If one was purchased at a particular temple and the wish has not come true, the owner can return it there for burning. Burning usually occurs at the year's end as a purification ritual to let the *kami*, or spirit within the daruma, know that the owner did not abandon the wish, but will persevere in the next year to make it come true.

FOR SEX AND FERTILITY

The human preoccupation with sex and love fuels the continued use of sex amulets and talismans throughout the world. Charms to attract sex and love and to increase fertility have been found in all cultures dating back to antiquity. For example, penis amulets were common in the late Roman era and examples have been found in a spring at an old Roman settlement near York in England. In ancient times, these charms were used as offerings to gods and were tossed into holy wells or springs as a wish for children or for luck in sexual conquests.

PERUVIAN LOVE CHARMS

The *munachi* is a Peruvian amulet used to cast sexual or love spells. *Munachi* is a Quechua word that combines *muna*, meaning "to desire" or "to love," with *chi*, meaning "to cause to happen." A *munachi* is a small, simple soapstone carving of a

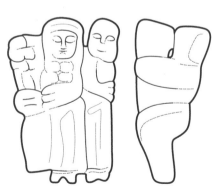

man and a woman engaged in sexual intercourse. A love spell is cast by wrapping a hair from the actual man and woman around the necks of the *munachi* lovers. The *munachi* is then buried in front of the door of the newlyweds' house.

Munaiwarmi means "woman's love stone" in the Quechua language. The *munaiwarmi* is a small carving depicting a woman holding flowers and a man standing next to her, symbolizing a happy marriage and the potential for children. Quechua women use this amulet to ensure their husbands remain faithful when they are away from home. As with the *munachi*, the *munaiwarmi* is wrapped with a lock of hair from both the man and the woman. The woman may keep it with her or she may give it to her husband to help him resist temptation.

AMERICAN BUCKEYE

In the midwestern United States, men may carry the buckeye in their pockets as a "lucky piece" to encourage good fortune in sexual encounters. The buckeye—also known as the horse chestnut—is a dark-brown nut with a very shiny, polished skin and a dull, pale-brown scar where it attached to the inside of the seedpod. The buckeye is so named because it resembles the eye of a buck deer. As a sexual charm, it is a potent symbol, in miniature, of firm, smooth testicles.

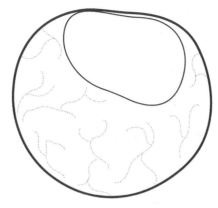

THAI PENIS AMULET

The Thai name for a penis amulet is *palad khik*, which means "honorable surrogate penis." Boys and men wear these small amulets under their clothes next to their penis to protect it from real or magical injury. The origin of the *palad khik* is the Indian Shiva lingam (see page 111), which was brought to Thailand by Cambodian monks in around the 8th century CE. The early examples of *palad khik* are inscribed with praises to Shiva (see page 116), while contemporary ones feature praises to Buddha. *Palad khik* amulets continue to be made by Thai Buddhist monks.

FOR HEALING AND THANKS

While many amulets and talismans are apotropaic—that is, they ward off evil—charms are meant to attract good luck and prosperity. The *milagros* and *ex votos* of Mexico are dedicated to healing: either asking for healing or giving thanks for it to God, Jesus, Mary, or one of the saints in the Catholic tradition. The charming and heartfelt paintings known as *ex votos* traditionally include a handwritten paragraph giving details about the person and the specific difficulty that either requires intervention or has been relieved. They function as visual and written prayers and are hung in the parish church of the supplicant.

MEXICAN MILAGRO

Milagros are small silver or gold votive offerings in the shape of arms, legs, eyes, or other body parts, or shaped as animals, fruits, or vegetables. They are offered to a favorite saint as a visual symbol of the petitioner's need for healing or in thanks for a prayer answered. *Milagros* are often attached to statues of saints or to the walls of churches in Mexico. For example, if someone has a broken arm, a tiny silver arm is hung on or near the favorite saint as a prayer for healing.

Milagros can be custom-made by a silversmith or purchased from a vendor outside the church. Their use represents an ancient custom of the Hispanic world, beginning with the Iberians of Spain in the 5th century BCE. Later, *milagros* accompanied the Spanish into the New World as votive offerings. The use of *milagros* continues to be an important part of folk culture throughout Mexico, New Mexico, rural areas of Spain, and other parts of the Mediterranean.

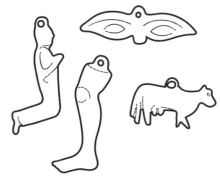

MEXICAN EX VOTOS

Ex voto is a shortened form of the Latin phrase *ex voto suscepto*, meaning "from the vow made." *Ex votos* are therefore an offering made to a saint or divinity in fulfilment of a vow or simply in gratitude for prayers answered. They can take many forms, but the most famous are small detailed biographical paintings, created on tin or wood, illustrating the circumstances of the supplicant's vow.

Usually executed in a primitive style, the painting may include the person making a vow and the saint or deity petitioned, as well as a paragraph or more of handwritten explanation. For example, the supplicant may promise to give up drinking if his child will be healed or his house will be rid of rats. The text may express this wish, or give thanks for the miraculous healing of the child or the miraculous arrival of a strange cat that exterminated the rats. *Ex votos* are placed in the church or chapel where the worshipper seeks help or wishes to give thanks.

ALPHABETS AND LETTERS

Ω

Western scholars postulate that the first alphabet appeared in Mesopotamia, possibly with the Assyrians, whose god Nebu is said to have revealed the cuneiform script to them. Hindus claim that the source of writing lies in India, with the ancient script of the Harappan civilization, but the Chinese assert that it is their written characters that are the oldest on earth. The truth is hidden in antiquity. But for all these ancient cultures, writing—whether used for mundane or religious purposes—was always a divine activity because it was used to convey the mysteries of the gods.

GREEK ALPHABET

The Greek alphabet, considered by many to be the first alphabet, is composed of 24 letters and has been used for writing the Greek language since the late 9th century BCE. It is the oldest alphabet in continuous use. Besides being used for writing modern Greek, its letters are used as symbols in mathematics and science. For example, astronomers use lower-case letters for naming the brighter stars in a constellation, while physicists use the Greek letter Lambda to represent wavelength and Omega to represent electrical resistance in ohms.

A α

ALPHA

B β

BETA

Γ γ

GAMMA

Δ δ

DELTA

E ε

EPSILON

Z ζ

ZETA

H η

ETA

Θ θ

THETA

I ι

IOTA

K κ
KAPPA

Λ λ
LAMBDA

M μ
MU

N ν
NU

Ξ ξ
XI

O o
OMICRON

Π π
PI

P ρ
RHO

Σ σ
SIGMA

T τ
TAU

Y υ
UPSILON

Φ φ
PHI

X χ
CHI

Ψ ψ
PSI

Ω ϖ
OMEGA

WESTERN MAGICAL ALPHABETS

In the West, from the 4th century CE until the 19th century, magical alphabets were created to communicate esoteric and mystical information or for political reasons, enabling indigenous peoples to communicate outside the Roman Latin of their rulers.

ANGELIC ALPHABET

Heinrich Cornelius Agrippa (1486–1535) created the Angelic alphabet during the 16th century for the purpose of communicating with angels. Also known as the Celestial alphabet, it is derived from the Greek and Hebrew languages.

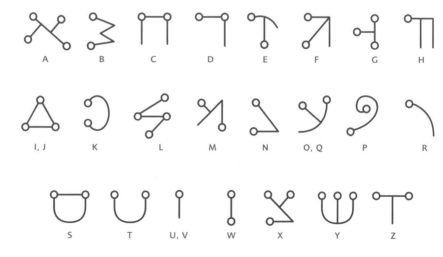

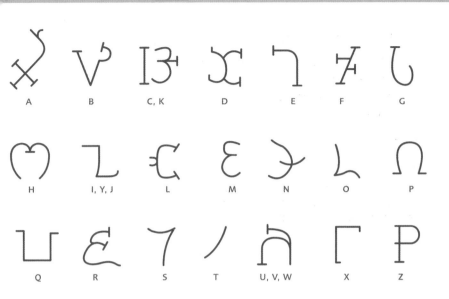

A   B   C, K   D   E   F   G

H   I, Y, J   L   M   N   O   P

Q   R   S   T   U, V, W   X   Z

ENOCHIAN ALPHABET

Dr. John Dee (1527–1608), magician and court astrologer to Queen Elizabeth I of England, and his colleague Sir Edward Kelly created this alphabet during the 16th century. Dee and Kelly claimed that angels gave them the alphabet and the Enochian language. Enochian magic was involved in the practice of invoking angels and was also central to the late 19th- and early 20th-century Hermetic Order of the Golden Dawn system of magic that was espoused by Aleister Crowley (see page 216).

MALACHIM ALPHABET

The Malachim alphabet, like the Angelic alphabet (see page 354), is derived from the Hebrew and Greek alphabets and was created by Heinrich Cornelius Agrippa during the 16th century. It is still used occasionally by Freemasons today.

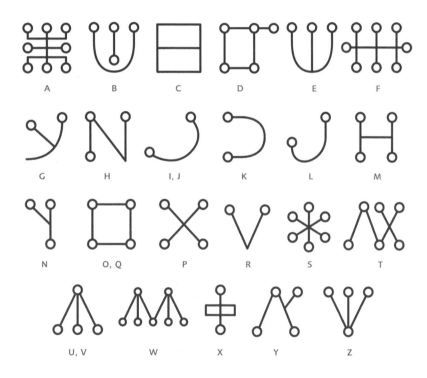

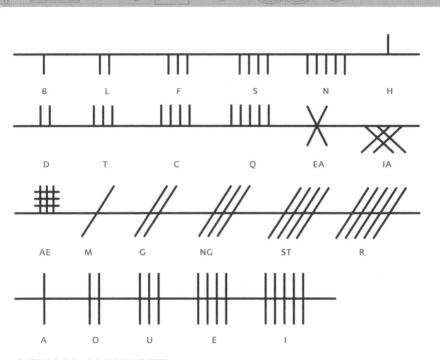

OGHAM ALPHABET

Inscriptions written in the Ogham alphabet have been found in Britain and Ireland dating from the 4th century CE. While all surviving examples of Ogham are inscriptions found on stone, it was probably more commonly inscribed on sticks, stakes, and trees. One theory concerning its origin is that it was designed by the Irish so as not to be understood by those who read the Latin alphabet—that is, the authorities of Roman Britain. A second school of thought believes that Ogham was invented by the first Christian communities in early Ireland, out of a desire to have a unique alphabet for writing short messages and inscriptions in the Irish language—the sounds of primitive Irish being difficult to transcribe into Latin.

PASSING THE RIVER ALPHABET

Heinrich Cornelius Agrippa also created the Passing the River (or *Passage du Fleuve*) alphabet during the 16th century. It is derived from a Hebrew alphabet used by early Kabbalistic rabbis. The river alluded to is the Chebar, which was located in central Babylonia, beside which captive Jews were settled.

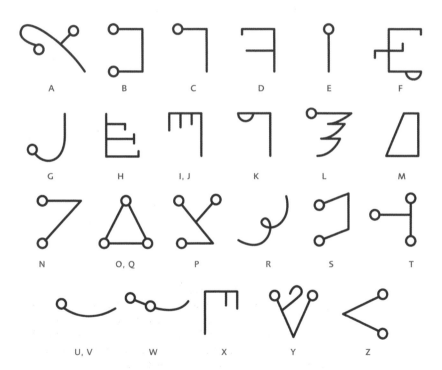

A	B	C	D	E	F
G	H	I, J	K	L	M
N	O	P	Q	R	S
T	U, V	W	X	Y	Z

END

THEBAN ALPHABET

The Theban alphabet was first published in Johannes Trithemius's *Polygraphia* of 1518, in which it was attributed to Honorius of Thebes. It is also known as the Runes of Honorius, although Theban is not a runic alphabet. Another name is the witches' alphabet, due to its use in modern Wicca and witchcraft as a cipher to hide magical writings from the uninitiated.

EASTERN SACRED SEED SYLLABLES AND WORDS

Sanskrit seed syllables and words, which are used in contemporary Hindu and Buddhist religious practice, stem from the ancient idea of spoken and written language as a sacred activity. The seed syllables and words function as symbols or aspects of divine or enlightened energy, which cannot be communicated in ordinary language. Entire texts have been written on the meaning of the sacred word/letter Om—a syllable that encapsulates the meaning of the combined syllables of the mantra *Om Ah Hum*, representing the body, speech, and mind of enlightenment. Each Sanskrit seed syllable is a symbol in its own right of vast spiritual meaning. Chanting the seed syllables within mantras and meditating on their meaning hastens realization of the spiritual truths contained within.

A

A is the seed syllable for Vairocana, one of the five esoteric forms of the historical Gautama Buddha. Buddha Vairocana embodies the Buddhist concept of *shunyata*, or emptiness. A is the primordial sound that comes with the out-breath and is the first letter of most alphabets. It symbolizes eternity, bliss, and the selfless nature of emptiness that pervades all beings.

AH

Ah is the seed syllable of Buddha Amoghasiddhi, another of the five esoteric Buddhas. Amoghasiddhi represents the path of fearlessness in confronting those things that are most difficult to address in oneself. Ah represents the throat chakra and the transformation of ordinary speech into pure or enlightened speech. It also occurs in the mantra *Om Ah Hum*.

DHIH

Dhih is a seed syllable symbolizing perfect wisdom—the wisdom that sees everything as it truly is. Dhih is associated with the bodhisattva Manjushri, who is depicted wielding an upraised flaming sword in his right hand, representing the wisdom that cuts through ignorance. In his left hand he holds a flower upon which rests the *Prajnaparamita Sutra*, another symbol of wisdom and attainment of enlightenment.

HRIH

Hrih is the seed syllable of Buddha Amitabha, one of the five esoteric manifestations of the Buddha, and is a symbol of love and compassion. In Tibet, Hrih is also associated with Chenresig/Avalokiteshvara, the bodhisattva of compassion. Amitabha is the main Buddha of Japanese Pure Land Buddhism and his seed syllable can be found everywhere in Japan.

HUM

Hum is the seed syllable that is associated with Buddha Askhobhya and represents truth and the mind. In Buddhist thought, Hum is the antidote to the false views of nihilism and eternalism. The truth that things are neither permanent and real, nor unreal and meaningless, reflects the Buddha's fundamental insight into the nature of phenomena.

MAIM

Maim (rhymes with "sign") is the seed syllable of Maitreya. Known in Buddhist tradition as the Future Buddha, Maitreya is a bodhisattva, an individual close to becoming a Buddha. Maitreya is prophesied to preside over a future age of enlightenment. His seed syllable Maim symbolizes the virtues of loving kindness and vigor gained through the practice of fearless compassion. Maitreya currently resides in the Tusita heaven, which is said to be reachable through meditation.

OM

Om (or OM), a sacred syllable in Buddhism, Hinduism, Jainism, and Sikhism, is known as the "jewel mantra" in Tibetan Buddhism and represents the body. It is pronounced A-U-M, expressing the combined seed syllables of Om, Ah, and Hum (see page 360). By itself, Om can represent body, speech, and mind or the basis of all existence. It is used at the beginning of many Buddhist and Hindu mantras. Its representation in the Devanagari script (see page 125) is better known than the Tibetan Uchen version shown here.

TAM

Tam is the seed syllable of the female Buddha Tara, an embodiment of love, kindness, and compassion in Tibetan Buddhism. Tara is often depicted as a beautiful young woman sitting on a lotus and moon cushion, with a moon halo around her (see page 10). Her right hand forms the giving *mudra* or hand gesture (see page 142) and her left forms a protection *mudra*. She holds an *utpala*, or lotus flower, as a reminder that worldly happiness is not satisfactory and that we must aspire to the joy of liberation.

TRAM

Tram is the seed syllable of the Buddha Ratnasambhava and represents generosity. He is associated with wealth and riches but not in the worldly sense, as his source of wealth is enlightenment. Meditation on Ratnasambhava is said to bring about a shift from a poverty mentality to one of abundance and a transition from a materialistic perspective to a spiritual one.

PHAT

Phat is a word that is pronounced as a single syllable, but actually written as two characters. In Buddhist mantras it functions similarly to a seed syllable and is often associated with the mantras of wrathful deities. *Phat* means "crack!"— or the sound of something cracking. It is said at the end of mantras to subdue demons or the forces working against enlightenment. It appears in the 100-syllable mantra of Vajrasattva, a bodhisattva associated with purification.

SOHA

Soha or *svaha* is not a seed syllable per se, but a word that is used to end Buddhist mantras that means "lay the foundation." In the mantra of Tara—*om tare tuttare ture soha*—*om* means the "body, speech, and mind" of Tara; *tare* represents Tara; *tuttare* means "one who liberates from fear"; *ture* means "one who liberates from illness"; and *soha* means "to lay the foundation or create the conditions so the supplicant will become like Tara herself."

TIME, SHAPE, NUMBER, AND COLOR

Concepts of time, shape, number, and color enable us to communicate and create. Measuring time gives humans some feeling of control over their lives and the ability to make plans. Shapes carry archetypal meaning and symbolize aspects of our world, communicating meaning on their own and adding meaning to other complex symbols. In sacred geometry, the proportions, shapes, or symmetries of a form have special significance, while from ancient times numbers have been seen as keys to the mysteries of the cosmos. Color is also associated with different secular and religious meanings.

TIME

The desire to measure time probably began with the realization that the sun rose in the east and disappeared in the west, only to reappear in the east the following morning. The earliest clock was probably the moon, which enabled hunter-gatherers to match the passing of the seasons with its phases. From this early time-keeper, more sophisticated methods of measuring time evolved.

SCYTHE

A curved blade mounted on a shaft, a scythe is used for mowing grasses. It may be held by the Greek god Chronus or the Roman god Saturn, both gods of time (the word "chronology" stems from the Greek *khronos*, meaning "time"). The scythe as an emblem of time cuts the thread of life and launches us one by one into eternity.

HOURGLASS

The hourglass represents the upper and lower worlds, the narrow opening showing the difficulty of transition between them. The hourglass stands for creation and destruction, life and death. The alchemical sign for hour was two semicircles on top of each other, as in the hourglass. In modern culture, the hourglass symbolizes the relentless passage of time, whether or not one notices its passage.

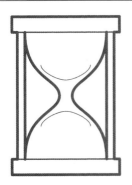

FATHER TIME

Father Time, who is usually depicted as an elderly bearded man carrying a scythe or hourglass (see opposite), is a symbol of passing time. He is sometimes paired with Mother Nature as a married couple. Father Time is a more modern version of the Greek Chronus and Roman Saturn (see opposite) and the Hindu Shani. In New Year traditions, such as greetings cards, Father Time personifies the old year who hands over the duties of time to the baby in diapers who personifies the new year.

GRIM REAPER

In Western cultures, death is often personified as the Grim Reaper and depicted as a skeleton carrying a large scythe and wearing a black robe with a hood. In some tales, the Grim Reaper is said to actually cause the victim's death, leading to stories that he can be bribed or outwitted, thereby delaying the inevitable. In other stories he is a psychopomp, a spirit who severs the final tie of the soul to the body and guides the deceased to the next world. The character Death has appeared in many novels, plays, and films over the centuries.

SHAPE

Shapes like the triangle, circle, square, and spiral form the foundations of mystical symbolism. The dynamic shape of the circle is found everywhere in nature and represents the union of the earth and heaven. Unlike the circle, the square is a man-made form that symbolizes stability and the earth. The zigzag is a primal shape that has had numerous symbolic meanings, while the cross within a circle is believed to be one of the most ancient symbols in the world.

TRIANGLE

The triangle is a symbol of ethics as it suggests mathematical exactness and method applied to spiritual problems. The triangle is a symbol for truth, the key to science and wisdom. Its study leads to revelations of the mystery of life.

The equilateral triangle is associated with the divine number three that in Christian symbolism stands for the Holy Trinity (see page 83). Philosophically, the triangle symbolizes the thesis giving rise to its antithesis, and these two together creating a synthesis. It is through the tension of opposites that something new is created.

The triangle is a symbol for power and as such relates to danger, but it also means safety and sometimes success and prosperity. For the ancient Hittites, the triangle was used to convey a meaning of well, good, or healthy.

In the eastern Tantric tradition, one of the symbols used for representing the female principle is a triangle (see page 128). This tantric triangle represents the vulva or yoni, or possibly the womb.

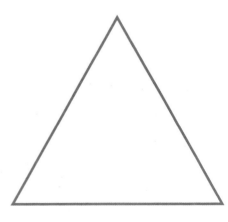

CIRCLE

The circle is a symbol found in all cultures throughout all ages and may have been the first shape drawn by humans. The circle symbolizes the sun—essential for life—as well as wholeness, completeness, illumination, the cycle of life, death, and rebirth, the Wheel of Life (see page 129), the Philosopher's Stone of alchemy (see page 188), and, in many religious traditions, the all-seeing or all-knowing eye. The circle has no beginning or end, so it is a universal symbol of eternity, perfection, divinity, infinity, and the cosmos. This shape symbolizes time and the cycles of the natural world, the moon, the planets, and the zodiac.

The circle also represents unity and is often used to signify and promote equality, as in the circular-shaped United Nations Assembly or the Round Table of King Arthur. For many cultures, the circle had magical functions symbolizing protection and the creation of a magical boundary that could not be crossed. In jewelry, the protective circle takes the form of a ring, bracelet, necklace, belt, or crown.

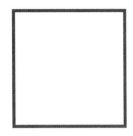

SQUARE

The square represents the earth and that which is created, as opposed to the circle (see page 371), which represents heaven and uncreated, primordial energy. The square symbolizes the physical world and space because it can reside on both the horizontal and vertical planes. In Buddhism, the square forms the base of the stupa (see page 126) and represents the earth. This shape functions as the archetype of order in the universe and the standard of proportion—the square being equal on all sides and angles. The expression "four-square" means one marked by firm, unwavering conviction, and promises stability and permanence.

To Pythagoras in the 6th century BCE, the square represented perfection. In Christian art, it refers to the Four Evangelists. Hindu or Buddhist mandalas that are images of the cosmos are often pictured as squares, with gates representing the four cardinal directions. In China, the earth was viewed as square and the square was an imperial emblem because the emperor was Lord of the Earth. The square signifies land, field, ground, or the element earth. In modern meteorology, it represents the ground.

CUBE

The cube—a square in three dimensions, with each face identical to the others—represents truth as, no matter which way it is viewed, it remains the same. Because it cannot be rotated, it symbolizes stability. In Islam and Judaism, the cube represents the core of the faith. The Kaaba (see page 106), the holiest shrine in Mecca, is constructed in the shape of a double cube. In early Kabbalist scriptures it is said that the angel Metatron created an elaborate talisman out of his own soul, which was based on the shape of a flattened cube. Considered a holy glyph, it was often drawn around an object or person to ward off demons and satanic powers.

LABYRINTH

As a shape, the labyrinth is a winding form that folds back on itself, with a single path leading to the center and back. Labyrinths are represented symbolically as drawings or physically on the ground, where they can be walked from their entry points to the center and back out again. They have historically been used in both group rituals and for private meditation. The labyrinth symbolizes a psychological or spiritual journey to the center of one's psyche or soul, to experience insight and then return to the everyday world transformed. (See also pages 49 and 53.)

SPIRAL

The spiral is common in the natural world, appearing in both the plant and animal kingdoms. Not surprisingly, the spiral is one of the most ancient symbols and features frequently in megalithic art, notably in the Newgrange passage tomb in Ireland (see page 52). Its appearance at other burial sites around the world suggests that the spiral was a universal symbol for the cycle of life, death, and rebirth. It may also have signified the sun, which appeared to die each night and be born again each morning. Ancient Chinese roof tiles were often decorated with the spiral. The spiral as a lunar, fertility symbol was often engraved upon Palaeolithic images of goddesses. On a cosmic level, it represented the cyclical nature of life and the reality of the constant dynamic movement of all things.

In ancient Celtic symbolism, a loosely wound counterclockwise spiral stood for the summer sun, while a tightly wound clockwise spiral symbolized the weaker winter sun. Double spirals signified the equinoxes. Spirals woven on carpets or cloth were believed to provide magical protective powers.

ZIGZAG

The zigzag is a primal shape that has had many symbolic meanings. The ancient Babylonians made use of it as a symbol of lightning. Their god of storms and wind, Adad, was depicted holding a zigzag in his hand. Neolithic bone fragments found in France dating back 300,000 years were also inscribed with zigzags, possibly symbolizing water or snakes.

In ancient Egyptian hieroglyphs a zigzag symbolized water and the zigzag is a symbol of the zodiac sign of Aquarius (see page 207). The letter S in the Norse runic alphabet is in the shape of a zigzag or lightning flash (see page 57). In modern times, a zigzag near electric installations indicates danger of electrocution. In Ghana, the zigzag, known as *owo akoforo adobe* or "snake climbs a palm tree," represents the exercise of wisdom, tactfulness, and prudence. The zigzag symbol is carved on the President of Ghana's Chair of State. The zigzag is also found on African kente cloth designs.

CROSS

The solar cross, or cross within a circle, is probably one of the oldest symbols in the world (see page 51). It represented the sun and the recurring cyclical nature of the seasons, and has appeared in Asian, American, European, and Indian art from the dawn of history. After losing its rim, it appeared as a four-armed free-standing cross, which was used to show the shadows cast by the rising and setting sun at the summer and winter solstices. A six-armed cross depicted the sunrise and sunset shadows of the equinoxes.

As an archetypal shape or symbol, the four-armed cross also represents the world axis, *axis mundi*, or the great pole around which the different constellations of the zodiac revolve. As the mystic center of the cosmos, the cross became a vehicle through which humans could access the divine realms. The cross is a combination of two different signs that symbolize the dual nature of human concerns, the marrying of the physical and the spiritual and of active and passive energies. The vertical axis (the upright pole or symbolic ladder) of the cross represents the spiritual impulse to reach the divine, while the horizontal crosspiece represents worldly or temporal concerns.

SACRED GEOMETRY

In sacred geometry, the proportions, shape, or symmetry of a form create harmonious structures that are not only pleasing but also connect with the larger energies of the universe. The golden ratio is one example of sacred geometry, used by Leonardo da Vinci (1452–1519) and many others in paintings, sculpture, city planning, and architecture. The Fibonacci sequence is another example that many plants and animals naturally embody as they grow.

GOLDEN RATIO

The golden ratio—which is also known as the divine proportion or golden mean—is represented mathematically as 1:1.618 and is often denoted by the Greek letter Phi (see page 353). It appears in nature as well as in man-made designs. Mathematicians, such as Pythagoras and Euclid in ancient Greece, the medieval Italian Leonardo of Pisa (see opposite), the Renaissance astronomer Johannes Kepler, and present-day Oxford physicist Roger Penrose, have been fascinated by the golden ratio. Biologists, artists, musicians, historians, architects, psychologists, and even mystics have marveled at the golden ratio's worldwide prevalence and appeal.

Since the Renaissance, many artists and architects from around the world have used this ratio in creating their works, because it was thought to be aesthetically pleasing. For example, the Greek sculptor Phidias (c. 490–430 BCE) seems to have used the golden ratio in creating the statues at the Parthenon in Athens. The Great Mosque of Kairouan reveals the golden ratio throughout its design. And the shape of the Great Pyramid at Giza in Egypt is very close to the proportions of the golden ratio.

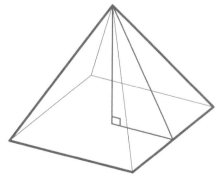

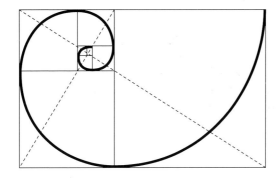

THE FIBONACCI SEQUENCE

Leonardo of Pisa (c. 1170–1250), the Italian mathematician known as Fibonacci, discovered a unique sequence of numbers that came to be termed the Fibonacci sequence. The series begins with zero and one, and then the previous two numbers are added together to get the next number, thus: 0, 1, 2, 3, 5, 8, 13, 21, 34, 55, 89, 144, etc. In 1202, in his book *Liber Abaci*, or *The Book of Calculations*, Fibonacci introduced the sequence to Western European mathematicians.

Previously the Indian grammarian Pingala had described the sequence in his book on prosody (the metrical structure of verse), written around 450–200 BCE. Prosody was important for ancient Indians, who placed emphasis on the purity of speech. The Indian mathematician Virahanka (6th century CE) and the Jain philosopher Hemachandra (1089–1172 CE) continued the work, showing how the sequence related to the rhythmic structure of verse.

The Fibonacci sequence can be seen in the development of many plants and animals, including the spiral of nautilus seashells, sunflowers, daisies, and pine cones, which have a Fibonacci sequential number of growing points. Mathematically, the Fibonacci sequence is closely related to the golden ratio (see opposite).

NUMBER

The great mathematician Pythagoras (c. 580–c. 500 BCE) believed that numbers ruled the universe. For him, even numbers symbolized the feminine principle and cyclical movement, while odd numbers represented the male principle and fixed positions. Medieval scholars believed that numbers had a divine source and possessed mystical powers. Each of the numbers that follows has its own imagery and significance for different peoples across the world.

ONE

The number one symbolizes unity and the first, the best and the only. It also represents harmony and peace. One stands independently and cannot be divided. In Christian and in the other monotheistic religions, the number one represents the one God, indivisible. It also symbolizes the primordial beginning from which all things originate. The single standing stone, the erect phallus, and the staff represent the primal creativity of the number one.

TWO

Two represents yin and yang (see page 146), polarity, and the realm of opposites. It is the first number that can be divided and thus represents division and difference. This number is symbolic of the duality of day and night, sun and moon, good and evil, and the two aspects of Christ—divine and human. Pairs of guardian figures double the sense of protection, as in the pairs of lions that are sometimes used to decorate the entrances to temples and palaces.

THREE

This number has a holy connotation in many cultures and represents variations on the trio of heaven (or God), the earth (or the cosmos), and humankind. In Christianity, the Father, Son, and Holy Spirit make up the Holy Trinity (see page 83). The Hindu trinity is composed of the deities Brahma, Vishnu, and Shiva (see page 116). Buddhists take refuge in the Three Jewels (see page 132): Buddha, Dharma, and Sangha.

FOUR

Four represents solidity, the earth, and material things and is linked to the symbols of the cross (see page 377) and the square (see page 372). This number represents the four cardinal directions—north, south, east, and west; the four seasons—summer, autumn, winter, and spring; the four elements—air, fire, water, and earth. Alchemists honored the Divine Quaternity as a fundamental aspect of the completion of the Greater Work. Pythagoras communicated the ineffable name of God to his followers using the number four or the "geometric square."

FIVE

Standing in the middle of the first nine numbers, five is the number representing the center and harmony. In China, five is the number of the center—the ideogram of *wu* (five) being composed of a cross and the center symbolizing the five elements. Five is also thought to be the symbol of the human being, composed of two arms, two legs, and the head and body. It also represents the phenomenal world of the five senses.

VI SIX

Six symbolizes perfection as power, manifested in the form of six equilateral triangles within a circle. However, this number also incorporates within it the confrontation of two threes, with the potential of creating as much harm as good. In the Book of Revelation, six is the number of sin and it symbolizes the deification of the power of the state over God. St. Clement of Alexandria noted that the world was created in six days and in the six directions of space, which are the four cardinal directions, plus the nadir and zenith.

VII SEVEN

Seven is a magical number symbolizing the perfection of a complete cycle. Each of the four phases of the moon has seven days and 7 x 4 equals 28 days, or a complete moon cycle. The sum of the first seven digits (1 + 2 + 3 + 4 + 5 + 6 + 7) also equals 28. Seven symbolizes a dynamic wholeness. There are seven main chakras (energy centers) in the body and in Islam there are seven heavens, seven hells, and seven earths. There are also seven days in the Jewish Passover. On the seventh day, God rested after creating the world.

VIII EIGHT

Eight stands for balance. In Buddhism, the eight-spoked wheel symbolizes the Eightfold Path to Enlightenment (see page 135) and there are eight petals on the lotus on which the Buddha sits. There are eight trigrams in the Taoist I Ching (see page 148) and Eight Immortals (see page 152).

Many baptismal fonts in Christian churches are octagonal, because eight represents regeneration and renewal. The eighth day following the seven days of creation stands for the resurrection and transfiguration of Christ and therefore of the human race. The eighth card of older Tarot decks is Justice, which is a symbol of the final weighing and of balance.

IX NINE

Nine symbolizes ritual, gestation, and exertion in pursuit of completion. Demeter wandered for nine days in search of her daughter Persephone. A woman is pregnant for nine months. Nine is a symbol of fulfilment, a complete journey before returning full circle to the number one. Infinity may be expressed by repetitions of the number nine, such as 999,999,999 . . . In Chinese mythology, nine is the number of the celestial spheres, and therefore there were nine steps up to the emperor's throne. The Aztec king Nezahualcoyotl built his nine-story temple to match the nine heavens.

X TEN

For Pythagoras, ten was the universal divine number, the perfect number that provides the basis for the decimal system that may have evolved because humans can count to ten using the fingers and thumbs of both hands. In China, ten is known as a multiple (5 x 2) that expresses duality and motion and so represents both death and life. The Maya regarded the tenth day as unlucky because it was the day of the death god. St. Augustine saw the number ten as the perfect expression of the sum of seven and three. The Ten Commandments give three laws relating to the love of God and seven to the love of humans.

XI
ELEVEN

If ten is a complete, perfect number, then the number 11—which is one too many—stands for excess, extravagance, or promiscuity. This number also suggests conflict and ambivalence. It could mean the start of a new cycle or the unbalancing, collapse, or corruption of the number ten. The number 11 suggests an individual striking out alone, in a rebellious or even lawless way, outside and without relationship to the cosmic whole. In African esoteric traditions, 11 is related to women and fertility—women having 11 body openings and men only nine.

XII
TWELVE

The number 12 symbolizes the cycles of the universe and its divisions in time and space. The dome of heaven is divided into 12 sections, resulting in the 12 signs of the zodiac. The Assyrians, Jews, and other peoples divided the year into 12 months. The Chinese and others in central Asia introduced 12-year cycles, which, when multiplied by five, equal 60 years, the point at which the solar and lunar cycles converge. In Christianity, there are 12 apostles, and rose windows in cathedrals were often divided into 12 sections.

XIII
THIRTEEN

Since classical antiquity, the number 13 has been deemed unlucky and a portent of bad things to come. The Kabbalah identifies 13 evil spirits. The 13th chapter of the Book of Revelation describes the Antichrist and the Beast. The 13 at the Last Supper—the 12 apostles plus Christ—preceded the coming betrayal by Judas Iscariot. Numerologists consider the number 13 to operate generally outside the laws of the universe in an unharmonious, erratic, and marginal way. The ancient Aztecs used the number 13 to divide time and kept a 13-day week.

COLOR

In ancient civilizations, color held mystical power as a manifestation of light and the divine. It is widely acknowledged that color influences our mood and stirs the emotions; color can either attract or repel. Many cultures have devised systems of color with religious or secular meaning. The color of images of the divine in Hinduism and Buddhism, the use of color in Islam, and the tinctures of heraldry are just a few examples.

BLUE

Blue represents both the vast expanse of the sky above and the unfathomable depths of the sea below. As a color, blue is thought to be spiritual, infinite, empty, spacious, and eternal. This is the coolest, most detached, least substantive of all colors, and is said to dematerialize whatever it touches. For example, a wall painted light blue can seem to shimmer and disappear. Blue also represents transparency and the world of dreams. It is the color of that which is surreal and not of this world.

The Egyptians, who painted the scenes of the weighing of the souls with a light sky-blue background, considered it the color of truth.

The blue color of the Virgin Mary's robe suggests her detachment from worldly life. For Tibetan Buddhists, blue represents transcendent wisdom and emptiness. Royal blue is the color of Nut, the Egyptian goddess of the night, who represents wisdom. The Hindu gods Krishna and Vishnu (see page 117) are depicted with blue bodies to signify their divinity. The color blue also symbolizes the desire for purity and what transcends worldly life.

RED

Whether red is bright or dark makes a difference concerning what it represents. Bright red is the color of fire, blood, heat, and power, and as such is a symbol of the life force. Throughout Asia, bright red is a lucky color. Buddhists consider it the color of activity and creativity. In Japan only children and women wear bright red. It is also the hue that appears on flags, stop signs, and emergency buttons, indicating danger. Christianity came to consider bright red as the symbol of lust and licentiousness and it was not favored; it was the color that represented martyred saints. Bright red is the color of romance, passion, youth, beauty, and emotion—a red-faced person is one who is angry or embarrassed.

Dark red, on the other hand, is seen as the red of spiritual initiation, of forbidden esoteric knowledge, of the blood inside the womb, of fire inside the earth, and of the mysteries of life. It is the color of the soul and the heart.

GREEN

Green is the color of nature, fertility, hope, renewal, and rebirth. In the Christian tradition, it symbolizes the triumph of life over death. Green is the liturgical color used during the celebration of the Epiphany and for the Sundays after Pentecost. It is a sacred color in Islam, representing fertility and spiritual knowledge (see page 107). Those who enter Paradise are said to wear green robes. In the West, green is the color of springtime and the start of a new life cycle. On a deeper level, it represents the hidden knowledge of the natural world. In China, green is connected to thunder and the arousing of yang energy (see page 146) in the spring. It corresponds to the wood element and represents longevity, strength, and hope. Modern marketing tests have concluded that green is the most neutral and tranquil of all colors.

Green also represents death and putrefaction. The greenish complexion of the sick contrasts with the life-giving promise of new and tender shoots of grass. In a rose window at Chartres Cathedral in France, Satan is depicted with green skin.

YELLOW

Yellow, representing the brilliant rays of the sun, is the hottest, most expansive, and intense of all colors. The color yellow symbolizes the gods, youth, and energy. In China, yellow is considered the color of fertile soil, as well as the imperial hue. In Tibetan Buddhism, yellow is the color of the earth element.

In other times and cultures the color yellow had less positive meanings. In medieval Europe, yellow was associated with deception and the doors of traitors' homes were painted yellow. In Chinese theatre, actors would paint their faces yellow to signify their character's cruelty and deceit. In Greek mythology, the golden apple was a symbol of love because Gaia had given it to Hera and Zeus as a wedding present; yet a golden apple called the Apple of Discord was a symbol of jealousy and pride and a cause of the Trojan War (see page 287). In Islam, golden yellow symbolized wise counsel, while pale yellow indicated treachery. Today, in the English language, yellow is associated with cowardice.

PURPLE

Purple became the color of royalty in the ancient world because purple dye was obtained from a scarce species of mollusk, making it very valuable. The Greek word for purple is *porphura*, referring to the name of the shellfish that was the source of the dye. Dark shades of purple continue to indicate wealth, royalty, nobility, and ceremony, whereas lighter shades are considered feminine and light-hearted. Purple also symbolizes spirituality, creativity, wisdom, and mystery. In the Book of Revelation, the color purple symbolizes both riches and the corruption of riches. In the Old Testament it also represented judges and judgment.

When it appears in nature—as in the flowers of the lavender, orchid, lilac, and violet—purple is considered delicate and precious. It is the color of mourning for widows in Thailand, and is used at later stages of mourning in the West (see page 306). The Purple Heart is a medal given to U.S. soldiers who have been wounded during combat.

BLACK

Black is the absence of light and is a sign of mourning in Islam (see page 107) and the Christian West. Throughout the world the color black is associated with evil, harm, and negative forces. Black is the color of night, adversity, and mystery. However, in mystical traditions, because it contains all colors, black is considered the color of the divine and the symbol of undivided oneness. In Islam, the veil of the sacred Kaaba at Mecca (see page 106) is black. In the Christian tradition, black is associated with penance.

WHITE

White can signify the absence of all color or the sum of all color. As such, it is simultaneously stillness, quiet, and potential, as shown in the white light of dawn. In the Christian tradition, white represents purity and virginity and is the liturgical color of Easter. White is the color of grace and divine manifestation and white haloes are often shown around the heads of those who have known the divine. In Islam, white symbolizes purity and peace (see page 107). However, Hindu widows wear white as a sign of their loss, because white is the color of mourning in Hinduism.

INDEX

ACKNOWLEDGMENTS

Executive Editor Sandra Rigby
Senior Editor Fiona Robertson
Executive Art Editor Leigh Jones
Designer Julie Francis
Illustrator Cactus Design and Illustration
Production Controller Linda Parry
Picture Researcher Claire Gouldstone

All photographs and illustrations are the copyright
of Octopus Publishing Group with the exception of
the following:

akg-images Erich Lessing 46, 314, Jean Louis Nou
133, Ulrich Sahm 263; **Alamy** Arco Images GmbH
51, Emma Wood 141, G P Bowater 391, Hoberman
Collection UK 176, Imagebroker/Stefan Auth 387,
ImageBroker/Walter G Allgower 280, 332,
Images of India 112, John Mitchell 349, Marc Hill
68, Mark Downey 384, Nano Calvo/Visual &
Written SL 169, North Wind Picture Archives 371,
Philip Game 17, The London Art Archive 165,
The Print Collector 175; **Ancient Art &
Architecture Collection** 25, 239; **Bridgeman
Art Library** British Museum, London 255, 338,
Fitzwilliam Museum, University of Cambridge 274,
FuZhai Archive 293, Leeds Museums and Galleries
(City Art Gallery) 18, Louvre, Paris 35, Musée de la
Vieille Charité, Marseille/Lauros/Giraudon 32,
Musée des Beaux-Arts, Tours/Lauros/Giraudon
237, Museum of Fine Arts, Budapest 186, National
Trust Photographic Library/Chris Gascoigne 77,
Palazzo della Ragione, Padua, Italy 15, Private
Collection 323, Royal Library, Stockholm 350, The
National Gallery, London 19, Valley of the Queens,
Thebes 230; **British Museum** The Trustees of the
British Museum 28; **Corbis** Atlantide Phototravel
91, Blue Lantern Studio 97, Bojan Brecelj 252,
Christine Kolisch 10, Courtesy of Museum of
Arqueologico Comarcal de Banyoles/Ramon Manet
377, David Samuel Robinson 383, Douglas Whyte
312, Fine Art Photographic Library 306, Frans
Lemmens/zefa 108, George McCarthy 302, Gianni
Dagli Orti 160, Jose Fuste Raga 366, Ladislav
Janicek/zefa 11, Mimmo Jodice 315 above,
Mohamed Messara/epa 373, Pierre Colombel 389,
The Irish Image Collection 380, Tom Grill 310;
Fotolia Benjamin Cabassot 58, Jeremy Richards
233, mpqphoto 315 below; **Heritage-Images**
E&E Image Library 40; **Lonely Planet Images**
Holger Leue 107; **Picture Desk** The Art Archive
296, The Art Archive/Culver Images 12; **Photo
Scala, Florence** 84, ArtMedia/HIP 129, Luciano
Romano 259; **Shutterstock** Mikhail Levit 72,
Ah Jin 130, Alex James Bramwell 388, DeshaCAM
209, HP Photo 390, iophoto 265, Jarno Gonzalez
Zarraonandia 67, Kim Pin Tam 9, Marie C Fields
287, Melissa Schalke 342, Nathan Chor 335,
Nick Poling 317, Robert Adrian Hillman 313;
SuperStock Fine Art Photographic Library 80,
Superstock, Inc 22; **TopFoto** Alinari 162,
Charles Walker 271, DPA/NMK/The Image Works
241; **Werner Forman Archive** Museum für
Volkerkunde 247, National Gallery Prague 250;
Wikipedia.com 114.